The Illustrated Guide to

TAROT

NAOMI OZANIEC

The Illustrated Guide to

TAROT

NAOMI OZANIEC

 A GODSFIELD BOOK

Library of Congress Cataloging-in-Publication Data Available

10 9 8 7 6 5 4 3 2 1

First paperback edition published in 1999 by Sterling Publishing Company, Inc.
387 Park Avenue South, New York, N.Y. 10016
© 1999 Godsfield Press
Text © 1999 Naomi Ozaniec

Distributed in Canada by Sterling Publishing
c/o Canadian Manda Group, One Atlantic Avenue, Suite 105
Toronto, Ontario, Canada M6K 3E7
Distributed in Australia by Capricorn Link (Australia) Pty Ltd
P O. Box 6651, Baulkham Hills, Business Centre, NSW 2153, Australia

Printed and bound in China

Sterling ISBN 0-8069-7091-X (trade)
ISBN 0-8069-7132-0 (paper)

The publishers are grateful to the following for permission to reproduce copyright material
Archiv für Kunst und Geschichte, London: 12, 15br, 21r, 48cl, 48b, 58cl, 67t, 70bl, 100tr, 104bl, 107br, 109br,
112. *The Bridgeman Art Library, London*: 23b, 62, 66bl, 83tl, 105r, 110tl. *Fortean Picture Library*: 16cl.
The Image Bank, London: 20b, 40b, 55t, 97tl, 114l, 115r. *Images Colour Library*: 79b.
N.A.S.A.: 74l. *The Stock Market, London*: 8tl, 21tl, 26, 34-35b, 38b, 54bl, 68b, 76b, 78, 80l, 82l, 85b, 110b,
123t, 126b. *Tony Stone, London*: 113tl.

TAROT CARDS
Illustrations from Egyptian Tarot, Golden Dawn Tarot, Herbal Tarot, Hermetic Tarot, Medicine Woman
Tarot, Medieval Scapini Tarot, Morgan-Greer Tarot, Motherpeace Tarot/Motherpeace Inc., Oswald
Wirth Tarot, Russian Tarot of St. Petersburg, Tarot of Marseilles (U.S. Games Systems/Carta Mundi),
Tarot of the Witches, Santa Fe Tarot, Ukiyoe Tarot, Visconti Sforza Tarot, Zolar's Astrological Tarot
reproduced by permission of U.S. Games Systems Inc., Stamford, CT 06902 U.S.A.

Illustrations from Aleister Crowley Thoth Tarot® reproduced by permission of AGM AGMüller,
CH-8212 Neuhausen, Switzerland. © AGM/OTO. Further reproduction prohibited.

Illustrations from the following decks reproduced by permission of HarperCollins Publishers Ltd:
The Angels Tarot (Robert Michael Place), The Greenwood Tarot (Mark Ryan and Chesca Potter),
Merlin Tarot (R.J. Stewart and Miranda Gray), The William Blake Tarot (Ed Buryn).

Zolar Tarot

Marseilles Tarot

Santa Fe Tarot

Egyptian Tarot

Motherpeace Tarot

Russian Tarot

Scapini Tarot

Golden Dawn Tarot

Hermetic Tarot

Santa Fe Tarot

Marseilles Tarot

Zolar Tarot

Russian Tarot

Motherpeace Tarot

Egyptian Tarot

Scapini Tarot

Golden Dawn Tarot

Hermetic Tarot

Contents

Introduction

ABOVE: *The mysteries of the Tarot are a fascinating treasure trove awaiting adventurous explorers.*

ABOVE: *The Major Arcana has 22 cards. These examples are from the Thoth Tarot.*

WELCOME TO THE TAROT

Encountering the Tarot for the first time is like opening a door into a new world or discovering a box of hidden treasure that has your name on it. The new world is full of discoveries just waiting to be made. The treasure trove is a box of great worth just waiting to be opened. However you see the Tarot, your encounter with it has the potential to change your life.

The Tarot as we know it today is made up of 78 cards. These are divided into two parts, the Major Arcana and the Minor Arcana. The Major Arcana consists of 22 trumps, a term derived from the Latin *trionfi* meaning "triumphs." This older term is more interesting than its modern derivative. It holds out promise and potential, whereas the term "trump" is related exclusively to card play. The term Arcana is derived from the Latin *Arcanum*, meaning a mystery or a secret. There is a subtle difference between these two definitions. A secret can be told or withheld, but a mystery can never be fully explained. Perhaps you might like to think of the Major Arcana as being composed of a number of triumphant mysteries. The Major Arcana brings you life-changing encounters at a profound level, while the Minor Arcana reflects the interactions of daily life, providing a context in which peak experiences take place. Together, the Major and the Minor Arcana present us with the images of life.

This book takes you on a journey into the Tarot, but at the same time it will take you on a journey into yourself. The Tarot always invites your participation and interaction. Each of the characters of the Major Arcana has something to say to you. Each has something to disclose or convey through dream or meditation, vision or revelation. These 22 characters are facets of your own nature as a fully rounded and developed human being. Your interactions will reflect the person you are.

ABOVE: *The Minor Arcana has 56 cards divided into four suits: Swords, Wands, Cups, and Disks.*

As you come to know the characters better, you will come to know yourself better. Observing yourself through the reflecting mirror of the Tarot provides an opportunity that is wholly yours.

This book is about opportunity. It provides suggestions and ideas that you may take up or modify, alter or interpret, according to your own light. Every suggestion is an opportunity for you to use, expand, and implement. The Tarot is entirely visual; it is a book of wisdom presented in pictures. The book offers you a wide variety of visual images, and these, too, are opportunities. Every Tarot image is a symbol that has a story to tell. Every story leads to a greater story that is the universal mythology of all times and places. This is the hidden treasure or the adventure in the new world, which you alone have the power to discover. If you allow the allow the Tarot to remain as a series of two-dimensional pictures, the living nature of the tradition will evade you. If you become engaged with heart and mind, body and soul, the Tarot will enter your inner life where it will become a trusty guide, a wise counsel, a reflecting mirror, and a source of endless and infinite creativity. If this is what you see, the Tarot welcomes you as it has always done.

Bring yourself just as you are, the Tarot awaits.

RIGHT: *Each suit has a King, Queen, Knight, and Page. This is the King of Cups from the Marseilles Tarot pack.*

ABOVE: *The Major Arcana consists of 21 characters. This is Strength, number VIII.*

The Birth of Tarot

THE PRESENT

Let us begin in the present, from where we may look back into the past. As we shall see immediately, the Tarot has shown itself to be a flexible system that has responded to differing places and times. Many of the 22 trump cards have been through various changes of name and place in the sequence. Today we know the characters of the Major Arcana as:

ABOVE: *In Tarot's early history, some of the characters were known by other names. The Hermit was called Father Time.*

RIGHT: *The Death card signifies change and new beginnings. This representation shows a skeleton; sometimes Death appears as a knight in armor riding a horse.*

0	The Fool
I	The Magician
II	The High Priestess
III	The Empress
IV	The Emperor
V	The Hierophant
VI	The Lovers
VII	The Chariot
VIII	Strength
IX	The Hermit
X	The Wheel
XI	Justice
XII	The Hanged Man
XIII	Death
XIV	Temperance
XV	The Devil
XVI	The Tower
XVII	The Star
XVIII	The Moon
XIX	The Sun
XX	Judgment
XXI	The World

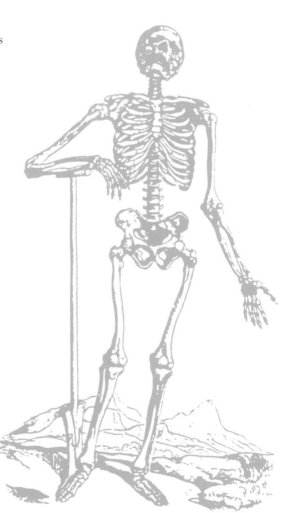

The first recorded sequence for the trumps is given in a sermon against gambling using dice, *Sermones de Ludo cum Aliis*, dating from 1500. Here we find some less-familiar names. The Tower is called the Arrow; Judgment is called the Angel; and the Hermit is called Father Time. This early manuscript also shows us a different order. The card of the Fool appears at the end of the series. The Empress is in second place and the Papess (the High Priestess) comes fourth, while Temperance is listed in sixth place. Even today, there is a small variation in order. The trumps Strength and Justice are sometimes interchanged, thanks to one of Aleister Crowley's revelations. As we shall see, the Tarot is the stuff of revelation.

ABOVE: *The order of the characters has changed during Tarot's history. The Fool is now at the beginning, though at one time appeared at the end of the series.*

The Minor Arcana consists of 56 cards divided into four suits traditionally called Wands, Disks, Cups, and Swords. The 20th century has baptized the Major Arcana with new and varied names, and recast the four suits in a variety of disguises. The Tarot has been redefined many times and is sure to undergo many more changes in the future.

ABOVE: *Cups correspond to Hearts in a deck of playing cards.*

ABOVE: *Swords correspond to the suit of Spades.*

ABOVE: *Disks (or Coins or Pentacles) correspond to Diamonds.*

ABOVE: *Wands (or Rods or Batons) correspond to Clubs.*

The Historical Roots

"Humanist philosophers, scholars, poets, painters, princes and churchmen in the Renaissance were in love with the civilizations of the ancient world."

RICHARD CAVENDISH,
The Tarot

THE SEARCH FOR ANCIENT WISDOM

The Tarot has a fascinating history that is well documented. Cards showing symbolic images appeared during the period now called the Renaissance, meaning rebirth. Though we are separated by 400 years, we share much in common with Renaissance thought. Currently we, too, live at a time of spiritual resurgence, redefinition, and transition. New Age ideas often hark back to a perceived ancient wisdom of earlier times. Renaissance minds were fired by a rediscovery of the classical world.

During the 15TH century, Italy opened itself to a new current that had its roots deep in the classical pagan past. In 1450 Cosimo de Medici commissioned the scholar, physician, and priest Marsilio Ficino to translate the works of Plato. He also commissioned the translation of the *Corpus Hermeticum*, which proved to be an intellectual and spiritual turning point for the whole of Europe. Ficino possessed an outlook that resonates with current metaphysical thinking. He was deeply interested in astrology, planetary influences, gemstones, and herbs. His own work, *The Book of Life*, is a compendium for constructing a life built upon cosmic principles. Ficino's approach was clearly ahead of his time. He advocated the use of images or mental pictures in a way that we might now call creative visualization.

THE REDISCOVERY OF CLASSICAL MYTHOLOGY

The classical revival created a new mindset. The past became a living resource to be tapped and recreated. Petrarch's poem *I Triumphi* was especially important. The poem describes the successive triumphal powers, Cupid, Chastity, Death, Fame, Time, and Eternity. Could there be a direct connection between Petrarch's inspirational poem and the depiction of 22 triumphal images? The poem portrays Petrarch and his beloved upon an image of the holy trinity set upon the figures of an ox, a man, a bull, and a lion. These four biblical images were to become the mainstay of the Minor Arcana.

This was a period in love with pageantry. Significantly, in the carnival festivities preceding Lent, the procession was opened by Bagatini, the Carnival King, and closed by the Fool. We can only wonder whether a creative mind of the time translated this spectacle into a painted image.

LEFT: *Tarot began life in the 14th century as a card game, Tarocchi, played just for fun.*

The Renaissance spirit provided the various ingredients in which creativity could thrive. Revisiting antiquity with artistic sensibility and spiritual hunger produced the seed that became the Tarot. It was fed by a rich classical stream of allegory, nurtured on a tradition of contemporary pageantry and formulated upon a newly found ancient mythology.

CARDS WITH TRIUMPHS

The Tarot was once a card game that was played for fun and entertainment. Playing cards containing the familiar four suits appeared in Europe in about 1377. Some 60 years later a new set of cards emerged known as *carte da trionfi*, "cards with triumphs." These cards contained a separate suit of Triumphs and included an additional picture card in each of the four suits. The earliest reference to this new type of card appears in the year 1442 in the account books from the court of Ferrara where the *Registro dei Mandati* mentions *pare uno de carte da trionfi*, cards with triumphs. The term *tarocchi*, which gave rise to the now familiar "Tarot," was first recorded in 1516. Had this term not come into general use, we might still be referring to these 78 cards as *carte da trionfi*.

POWERFUL PATRONS

We cannot ignore the contribution of the Visconti-Sforza families in the history of the Tarot. These two powerful Italian families commissioned 11 different sets of tarocchi cards. Of the original 11 sets, two sets remain almost complete, but four sets retain only a single card. It seems most probable that such packs were commissioned to honor significant events: the wedding of Filipo Visconti to Maria de Savoy in 1428, the wedding of Francesco Sforza to Bianca Maria Visconti in 1441, and Franceso's assumption of the ducal crown in 1450. A set of 16 hand-painted cards were even sent as a gift to Queen Isabella in 1449. Commissioned by Fillipo Maria Visconti, the cards depicted Virtue, Riches, Pleasure, and Virginity in the guise of classical divinities. Such gifts were part of the Renaissance exuberance. This was an age in love with art and allegory, display and divinities, patronage and paganism.

"Classical mythology became so familiar to educated men and women of the Renaissance that it could be used as an allegorical language to convey meanings not always obvious to modern eyes."

MARGARET ASTON,
The Panorama of the Renaissance

ABOVE: *Beautifully illustrated Tarot card sets were commissioned by the influential Visconti-Sforza families in 15th century Italy.*

ABOVE: *Antoine Court de Gébelin suggested that Tarot cards originated in* The Book of Thoth, *an ancient Egyptian book of magic.*

ABOVE: *Court de Gébelin connected the 22 letters of the Hebrew alphabet with the 22 trumps of the Tarot.*

The Redefinition of Tarot

THE TAROT AND THE PROTESTANT PASTOR

The seeds of the Tarot that had been firmly planted in the 15TH century were rediscovered in 1781 by Antoine Court de Gébelin, a Protestant pastor and freemason. He suddenly saw the Tarot in a new light and wrote:

"Imagine the surprise which the discovery of an Egyptian book would cause if we learned that a work of the ancient Egyptians still existed in our time ...
This Egyptian book does exist. This Egyptian book is all that remains in our time of their superb libraries. It is even so common that not one scholar has condescended to bother with it since no one before us has ever suspected its illustrious origin. The book is composed of seventy-seven, even seventy-eight, sheets or pictures divided into five classes, each showing things that are as varied as they are amusing and instructive. In a word this book is the game of Tarot."

The influence of his revelation lasted. It was Court de Gébelin who connected the 22 trumps of the Tarot with the 22 letters of the Hebrew alphabet. It was Court de Gébelin who recast the Papess as the High Priestess and the Pope as the Chief Hierophant, or High Priest. He called the Devil Typhon, identifying him as Set, the enemy of Osiris. He called the Star Sirius and the Chariot Osiris Triumphant. This new emphasis shifted the Tarot from the setting of one age to a mythic atmosphere. Court de Gébelin's own work, *Le Monde Primitif*, included an additional essay by an unnamed contributor who called the Tarot *The Book of Thoth*, a name that has endured into the 20TH century. Court de Gébelin had redefined the Tarot.

THE TAROT IN THE 19TH CENTURY

The French occultist Etteilla also saw an Egyptian hand at work within the Tarot. He regarded the Tarot as a book of wisdom covering universal medicine, an account of creation and a history of mankind. He even claimed that the *Book of Thoth* was devised by a committee of 17 magi, and that the first copy was inscribed on leaves of gold. Etteilla's writings on numerology, alchemy, astrology, and most especially on the Tarot as a form of fortune-telling, resulted in a surge of interest in the drawing rooms of Paris.

Etteilla was followed by another French occultist, Eliphas Levi, who took the Tarot even further into mystery and magic through Qabalistic, Hermetic, alchemical, and ancient references. He related the Tarot to the Qabalah. It was a marriage of systems that has lasted to this day. By now, the Tarot had become identified with magical orders, secret societies, and spiritual élites. Society at large had no interest in such esoteric activities.

The inspired recreation of the Tarot was completed in England by The Hermetic Order of the Golden Dawn. Several significant decks were produced during this time, including the Golden Dawn's own Tarot, the now popular Rider-Waite Tarot, and Crowley's deck, which he called The Book of Thoth. It was here that the Tarot was incorporated into a magical, philosophical, and spiritual system. This rich legacy has served the 20TH century ever since.

THE TAROT IN THE 20TH CENTURY

The Tarot has undergone a complete revolution during the 20TH century. It began as a symbolic code to be explained only to the members of a closed metaphysical society. Members swore an oath not to reveal what was shown to them. Tarot packs were few in number – metaphysical bookstores were practically unknown.

The Tarot was once treated with a mixture of suspicion and derision. It was not taken seriously or valued outside the membership of closed spiritual groups. Meditation was practically unheard of at the turn of the century.

Western consciousness has changed so much in the intervening years. There has been upsurge of enthusiasm for the psychological and the spiritual. Visualization and meditation have become acceptable paths of knowing. Spiritual lifestyles have become common. The renewed interest in the symbolic images of the Tarot has emerged as part of a wider current of personal development. The Tarot is now for everyone who seeks it.

ABOVE: *Court de Gébelin declared that the four suits of the Tarot represented the strata of Egyptian society: nobility (Swords), agricultural workers (Wands), the priesthood (Cups), and commerce (Disks).*

BELOW: *A 16th-century fortune-teller uses a set of cards to reveal future events.*

Choosing Your Pack

ABOVE: *The Visconti-Sforza Pierpont Morgan Tarrochi deck originated in the 15th century.*

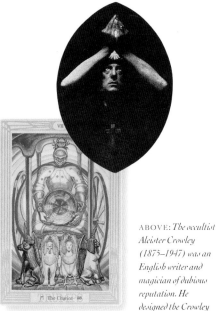

ABOVE: *The occultist Aleister Crowley (1875–1947) was an English writer and magician of dubious reputation. He designed the Crowley Thoth deck.*

SPOILED FOR CHOICE

Today there are so many Tarot packs, the choice can be quite overwhelming. However, as you will be the person using the deck, choose a pack that reflects something about you. The following categories provide a guide to some of the packs available. If you cannot make up your mind, try the Inspiration Tarot, which consists of 78 blank cards. It awaits your inspiration!

Historical Tarot

These decks are reproductions of historical packs. They are of great interest as they show us the Tarot rooted in a different age and time.

Ancient Tarot of Marseilles: A reproduction of the original 1760 pack.

Spanish–English Tarot: A deck based on woodcuts dating from 1736.

Ancient Minchiate Eturia: A reproduction of a Florentine deck from 1725.

Visconti-Sforza Pierpont Morgan Tarrocchi: A reproduction of the 74 existing cards plus four recreated ones. A particularly beautiful deck.

Cary-Yale Visconti Tarot: A facsimile reproduction from the manuscript library of Yale University. An unusual set containing 16 cards per suit.

Esoteric Ancient Tarot: A reproduction of a Parisian Tarot from 1870.

Classic Tarot

This category derives from the creative impetus of the Hermetic Order of the Golden Dawn. They have stood the test of time and acquired classic status.

Crowley Thoth deck: The deck designed by Aleister Crowley, who delighted in his own bad reputation. It features stunning artwork by Frieda Harris.

The Golden Dawn Tarot: Based on the collaborative work of MacGregor Mathers and his wife, the artist Moina Bergson.

The Rider-Waite Tarot deck: This has become probably the most popular of all Tarot decks. It presents a Qabalistic philosophy in a clear symbolic language. This Tarot has been closely emulated by other Tarot decks.

The Builders of the Adytum Tarot: Shares much in common with the Rider-Waite Tarot, but you color your own deck as a meditative practice.

The Zolar Astrological Tarot: Based on the Rider-Waite Tarot, but uses a standardized color code.

Goddess Tarot

Motherpeace Round Tarot: This popular contemporary Tarot deck, a celebration of women's culture, represents a complete redefinition of Tarot.

Gendron Tarot: Named after the originator, this Tarot takes you into the world of the goddess and her animal companions.

National Tarot

These packs draw upon national mythology and history, and are particularly appropriate if your ancestral roots tap into any of these traditions: *African Tarot, Mayan Tarot, Chinese Tarot, Russian Tarot of St. Petersburg, Ukiyoe Japanese Tarot, Norse Tarot, Kalevala Tarot* (based on Finnish epic poems).

Fantasy Tarot

The fantasy decks combine traditional Tarot format with characters drawn from the world of the imagination.

The Lord of the Rings Tarot: Enter the world created by J. R. R. Tolkien.

Dragon Tarot: A deck for dragon lovers everywhere.

Unicorn Tarot: The unicorn continues to fire the imagination.

Tarot of the Cat People: A deck for wild feline fantasists.

Mythological Tarot

These packs draw on a broad mythology that extends beyond national boundaries: *Celtic, Renaissance, Viking, Arthurian, Merlin.*

Hermetic Tarot

These decks reflect a particular philosophy and spiritual practice: *Tarot of Ceremonial Magick* (includes Enochian and tattwa symbols), *Tarot of the Sacred Rose, The Alchemical Tarot* (uses images from the alchemical tradition).

Fun Tarot

Tarot of Baseball: A new look at both baseball and the Tarot.

Wonderland Tarot: Alice's adventures through the looking glass of Tarot.

Tarot for Cats.

ABOVE: *The mysterious Hanged Man from the Golden Dawn deck, a classic Tarot pack.*

ABOVE: *Japanese Tarot draws on the meticulous, stylized artistic traditions of the East.*

17

How to Use this Book

BEGIN

This book is written to introduce you to the fascinating world of the Tarot. Its pages are filled with images that delight and interest the mind. The book invites your participation, for there is no other way to meet the Tarot except through interaction. Perhaps you have already encountered the Tarot; perhaps you have had a Tarot reading with someone; perhaps you know nothing about the Tarot and come with no expectations; perhaps you have heard about the Tarot and come with many preconceptions. No matter what you already know or believe, let this book take you on a journey of discovery.

OPEN

Let this book open the door into the world of the Tarot. Let it open your mind to possibilities and ideas about yourself and life in general. You do not have to work through the book in a particular order; just open it at any page and let the pictures and words filter gently into your mind. As you open yourself to the ideas that the Tarot presents, new possibilities and perceptions will open up to you. You will find yourself looking at your own life in a different way. Open your mind and let the Tarot in; you will be glad that you did.

ABOVE: *It can be interesting to keep a journal about your journey into the Tarot, recording experiences and revelations.*

RIGHT: *Tarot can reflect uncharted waters of the psyche and reveal new voyages to be made.*

EXPLORE

As you enter the world of the Tarot, you will doubtless want to explore its historical, cultural, and spiritual connections. Let this book take you on a voyage of discovery into mythology, psychology, astrology, comparative religion, and spiritual tradition. The religions, cultures and peoples of the world are here. You can develop any thread to see where it leads. Of course, as you become more familiar with the Tarot, you will discover that you are just exploring yourself.

INTERACT

This book invites you to interact. Keep your own Tarot journal. Record your thoughts, ideas, and inspirations. Keep records of the Tarot spreads that you do for people. This is not a workbook, but a joyful exploration of the many images of the Tarot – use it in the order that you choose. Each double page is a self-contained section, so you can combine sections in your own way.

Here you will find practical guidelines on meditation, working with symbols, visualization, and divination. Use the Seed Thoughts and Key Symbols as jumping-off points for the mind. Work with them as intensely or as loosely as you wish. Interact in your own way and at your own pace, but do interact. Perhaps you have already integrated meditation into your life, in which case you will need no further encouragement to meditate on the Tarot cards. Or perhaps meditation will be another new adventure – if so, let the Tarot take you toward it. Visualization is a way of waking up the mind and using its powers more effectively. As the Tarot is entirely visual, it provides a ready-made focus for this practice. Visualization and meditation are the keys that will unlock the doors of the Tarot for you. If you do not choose to apply them, the Tarot will remain as a two-dimensional series of pictures. Apply the keys and discover the difference.

ABOVE: *The Seed Thoughts on each spread are intended to germinate a practical, positive approach toward living.*

ABOVE: *The Key Symbols that are associated with each card of the Major Arcana offer some fascinating links.*

ENJOY

Enjoy as you learn. Enjoy the fact that the Tarot will broaden your horizons. Enjoy the new thoughts and insight that the Tarot will bring. Especially enjoy the images of the Tarot that will have their own special effect on you.

CONTINUE

This book is intended to open a door into the fascinating world of the Tarot. It is hoped that once you have glimpsed this world, you will want to explore more deeply on your own. Let this book become a stepping stone to a greater and deeper relationship with the Tarot that awaits you in the future.

The Language of Symbols

ABOVE: *The Soul of the World from the Angels Tarot pack. Western religious symbols frequently appear in many Tarot decks.*

READING PICTURES

We live in a literate society that reads any number of words, but has, for the most part, forgotten how to read pictures. The Tarot can be thought of as a book in symbolic pictures, and we need to learn its language. Each card is a treasury of symbolic images. Every symbol is a key that unlocks a deeper understanding. Every symbol is a doorway through which we may pass. Symbols are drawn from real life and have taken on an abstract meaning through a shared understanding.

Imagine for a moment that you have been given the task of conveying a simple message to a group of visitors from a number of different countries. In this scenario no one speaks your language. You have pen and paper. Perhaps you need to tell them to meet at a particular time, in which case you might naturally draw a clock, and perhaps a depiction of the meeting place. Simple messages are easily conveyed. Now imagine that your job is to convey a philosophy of life and death using only pictures. This is the Tarot.

THE LANGUAGE OF THE TAROT

Although there are many Tarot decks, there is only one language. The categories of symbols are derived from the work of Robert Assagioli, the founder of psychosynthesis. He placed great importance on the symbols as a means of psychological growth and personal well-being. If you already have a Tarot pack, see how many of these categories you can find. Recognizing these symbols is the first step. Decoding them comes next.

Natural symbols

Earth, air, fire, water, sky, stars, sun, moon, mountain, sea, stream, river, lake, pond wind, cloud, fog, tree, cave, flame, fire, wheat, seed, flowers, rose, lotus, sunflower, jewels, light, (sunrise, rays of light, darkness).

Animal symbols

Lion, tiger, bear, snake, wolf, deer, bull, goat, worm, chrysalis, butterfly, birds, domestic animals, the egg.

BELOW: *What do you think of when you see a butterfly? Lightness, transformation, new life, beauty?*

LEFT: *The lotus, sacred in Asia and the Orient, symbolizes love, the universe, rebirth, and enlightenment.*

Human symbols

Father, mother, son, grandfather, grandmother, son, daughter, sister, brother, child, wise old man, magician, king, queen, prince, princess, knight, teacher, the human heart, the human hand, the eye, birth, growth, death, resurrection.

Man-made symbols

Bridge, channel, reservoir, tunnel, flag, fountain, lighthouse, candle, road, path, wall, door, house, castle, stairway, ladder, mirror, box, sword.

Western religious symbols

God, Christ, holy mother, angels, devils, saints or holy men, priest, monk, nun, resurrection, hell, purgatory, heaven, the grail, temple, chapel, cross.

Eastern religious symbols

Brahma, Vishnu, Shiva, the Buddha.

Mythological symbols

Pagan gods and goddesses, heroes, Apollo, the Muses, the Three Graces, Venus, Diana, Orpheus, Hercules, Vulcan, Pluto, Saturn, Mars, Mercury, Jupiter, Wotan, Siegfried, Brunhilda, Valhalla, the Nibelungen, the Valkyries.

Teaching symbols

Wise man, old man, magician.

Abstract symbols

Numbers: As Pythagorean symbols.

Geometrical: Dot, cross, equilateral triangle, square, diamond, five-pointed and six-pointed stars.

Three-dimensional figures: Sphere, cube, cone, ascending spiral.

ABOVE: *Prince Siddhartha Gautama, the founder of Buddhism, was born about 600 B.C.E. One of many religious symbols to be found in the Tarot.*

Approaching the Symbols

ABOVE: *The Santa Fe Tarot uses the flat, angular shapes of traditional Navaho Indian art, together with its sacred tribal patterns and symbols.*

DECODING THE CODE

Having established the fact that the Tarot is a symbolic pictorial system, and in order to read its message, simply ask yourself: "What does this mean to me?" when meeting a symbol for the first time. There is no right or wrong answer. There is no single answer. There is no complete answer.

Some symbols are very easy to read because they are already part of our cultural or universal inheritance. For instance, we all have immediate responses to obvious symbols such as the sun or the moon, which are recognized worldwide. Other symbols have a more limited application, especially if they represent particular spiritual or national traditions. If appropriate, place yourself in the relevant cultural context of the deck you are using. The Santa Fe Tarot uses the symbols of the Navaho tradition. Mentally stepping into the shoes of the Navaho life will reveal the significance of clouds and lightning, stars and seeds, arrows and logs. The Russian Tarot uses symbols in a way that reflects Russian history. Many Tarot decks draw upon a broad historical and cultural base. For instance, the Motherpeace Tarot refers to the Goddess traditions of many ages and places. The wider your own background knowledge, the greater your understanding of the symbolic references will be.

Keep a Journal

It is a good idea to create a Tarot journal in which you record your insights into the meaning of each symbol. Try the following approaches to the symbols of your chosen pack.

BELOW: *Create a journal to note down symbols and what they mean to you: a reference work that will support your learning.*

Free Association

Write down everything that springs to mind in connection with the symbol you are working with. Brainstorm and record all your thoughts and ideas.

Historical References

Be aware that the symbols you are looking into are not new, but are often extremely old. You may even discover them in unexpected places. Some very

ancient symbols are in current use as company logos. You will find references in museums and libraries. Assemble as many old ideas about these symbols as you can find.

Compare and Contrast

Examine how your own thoughts compare to those of earlier civilizations. It may come as a surprise to find that your own thinking will probably be much along the same lines as that recorded by history.

Cross-References

Be aware of cross-references. As you discover more about the historical and spiritual uses of symbols, you will begin to find enormous interconnections across time and culture. You will also see how different Tarot decks employ the same symbols. No matter which Tarot deck you have chosen to work with, you will be able to identify many of the same symbols.

Building your Symbolic Vocabulary

These are approaches that strengthen your intellectual understanding of symbols. This is fascinating, but to get the most from the Tarot, especially for divination, we need to move from an intellectual understanding to an intuitive understanding. In other words, we need to be able to think naturally, easily, and quickly in symbols, and to do this we need to build an inner vocabulary. It is helpful to adopt a more systematic approach and to pass the symbols directly into the mind through visualization and meditation. When you begin to think symbolically, you may find a real a sense of mental expansion. When you move naturally into symbolic thought, you will experience a new way of understanding. Every symbol asks to be understood both intellectually and intuitively. When the symbols have become part of you, you will find that your mind is expanded and your vision of life extended.

ABOVE: *The Tower from the Motherpeace Tarot. This card symbolizes shocking events, destruction, and change.*

BELOW: *Native American shamanic cultures have a rich vocabulary of symbolism.*

Visualization

ABOVE: *To improve your memory of the cards, try focusing on key features. Here it might be the sword, scales, and colors.*

OPENING THE EYE OF THE MIND

Forging a relationship with the Tarot is not unlike forging a new friendship. We begin by wanting to become acquainted. We spend time together. We exchange ideas. We get to know each other. We listen and share. Then we move into a deeper and meaningful relationship. Real friendship is not possible without interaction. Befriending the Tarot is not possible without involvement. Just as we can easily call to mind the faces of family and friends, so we can learn to call to mind the faces and presence of the Tarot family. We do this through visualization. In other words, we recreate particular images within the mind by opening the mind's eye.

VISUALIZATION

Visualization is an important technique found at the roots of many different spiritual traditions. Creating mental images helps to develop concentration and unlock creativity. Spiritual art is rich in symbolic icons that are internalized through visualization and meditation. The Tarot images are no less sacred for being contemporary.

Visualization is a normal and natural practice, although your ability to visualize may need a little waking up. If you have never tried this before, you can start right now. Wherever you are, just spend a minute looking at your surroundings. Close your eyes and see how much you can recreate from memory and with how much success. How did you get on? How did you score on visual memory? Was your image clear and accurate, or hazy? When you are ready to apply your visual memory to the Tarot, try the following: take a card of your choice, close your eyes, and try to reconstruct it in the mind's eye. Open your eyes and check how successful you were. When you have mastered the principle, apply it to each of the cards as you study them.

LEFT: *The Moon card from the Russian Tarot. Which details will help you commit it to memory?*

Try your present skills on the following card: You might find that bits of an image disappear as soon as your concentration fades, or perhaps that the details are hazy. If so, try to include all the senses. It is impossible to imagine standing beside the sea without also hearing the sound of waves breaking on the shore – so use the imagination to create relevant scents, sounds, or tactile experience.

Don't restrict yourself to visualizing the Tarot images – use visualization in your everyday life. The more observant you are, the more you will bring to your Tarot studies. The cards often include natural imagery such as trees and flowers, streams and stones. Use your imagination to smell a rose or a lily, run your hand over the bark of a tree, dip your fingers in a flowing stream, or hold a cold pebble in your hand.

BRING THE TAROT TO LIFE

The sacred image has always played an important role in the development of a spiritual life. The Tarot symbols, like a carefully written sacred code, are designed to evoke a personal response. Visualization will bring the Tarot to life. Its symbols will become more than two-dimensional pictures for you. Visualizing the Tarot will turn cards into interior landscapes and characters into friends. The Tarot will come to life for you as an inner domain where you may interact, explore, and communicate. Try it and see for yourself.

ABOVE: *Link the image to your own experience of a full moon on a clear night, to lock it in your mind.*

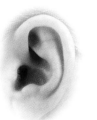

LEFT: *Use all your senses to help with recall during visualization, thereby enriching the details of the Tarot images.*

Sight   *Hearing*   *Smell*   *Touch*

Meditation

THE MEDITATIVE TRADITION

Meditation is probably the oldest spiritual discipline and the many themes, ideas, and images of the Tarot cry out for the deep interaction that is meditation. Meditative interaction with the Tarot will undoubtedly change you. You may already know a great deal about it, in which case you can proceed to use the Tarot as you wish. But if meditation is new, let us begin with the simplest of ideas. Think of meditation as a way of holding the mind on target. In other words, when we take a subject for meditation, we hope to think about it as deeply and constantly as possible in the time we have set aside. In practice, our thinking will probably be distracted because all sorts of other things just float into our minds. So the theory is simple, but the practice is a little more difficult.

Water

Air

SUBJECTS FOR MEDITATION

The following are suggested as subjects for meditation. It is a good idea to record the results of your meditative thoughts, to see how they progress over time.

- The name of each of the trumps
- The seed thoughts suggested for each trump
- The key symbols associated with each trump
- The element of earth
- The element of air
- The element of fire
- The element of water
- The element of *Akasa*

Earth

ABOVE: *Meditation takes many forms. Visualization is itself an important mental technique, so when meditation and visualization combine in the visualized meditation, it is quite different from an analytical reflective meditation (as shown in the example of the Seeker).*

Fire

UNDERSTANDING THROUGH MEDITATION

Here is a sample of reflective meditation where a single idea is explored. The subject of the meditation is the Seeker, which is the title of Tarot trump II, the High Priestess in the Medicine Woman Tarot.

LEFT: *The Seeker, or High Priestess from the Medicine Woman Tarot, can be used for a reflective meditation.*

"I hold the title Seeker in my mind and begin to explore what this means. Am I the seeker – what am I seeking, where will I find it, who will help me? I realize that all spiritual travelers have been called seekers – am I like them, like the questers of all times? What is that we all seek? My mind seems to drop into a deep place; there is a long pause as I ponder this question. What is it that I want? I realize that I want to know who I am. Is this what all questers have sought? Now I see an image of the path, and I see myself walking along, literally stopping at every stone, to look under it – so I will leave no stone unturned to find what I want. As I stand with a stone in my hand, I find that the path is full of people walking along all together. I don't know where they are going, but I just join them. Is that is what being a seeker means? I still don't know, but perhaps I will find out."

Visualized meditations draw upon the power of the mind to create mental images. However, their purpose is not merely to create a scene in the mind but to respond within it. The personal response can be surprisingly spontaneous and profound. This is the moment when the seeds of change are planted deep within you. The following is sample of a visualized meditation based on the Two of Cups in the Thoth pack.

BELOW: *The Two of Cups from the Thoth Tarot makes a good basis for a visualized meditation.*

Allow your surroundings to dissolve. Find yourself in a surreal landscape. You are floating in waters that are warm and buoyant. You feel totally supported here. Above you is an endless blue sky. Before you a double lotus has arisen from the depths. A strong green stem rises from the lotus. Two dolphins intertwine around the stem that supports a second lotus that blooms high in the air. Its petals are pale pink. A subtle perfume fills the air. It is reminiscent of the delicate perfume of a rose. From the bowl of the lotus two streams of water cascade toward you. Each stream bounces off one of the dolphins before it bridges forward toward you. Each cascading stream is captured in a chalice before it overflows. You reach out and dip your finger in each of the two chalices. You put your finger in your mouth and taste the waters. This water has a taste that is indescribably wonderful. You taste the blossom of the lotus, the depth of the sea, and the arc of heaven. Here is something wonderful and sublime; you reach out with cupped hands and take your fill until you have drunk all that you need.

After this kind of meditation, the scene fades and your attention returns to familiar surroundings. Write down your feelings in your Tarot diary.

The Tree of Life

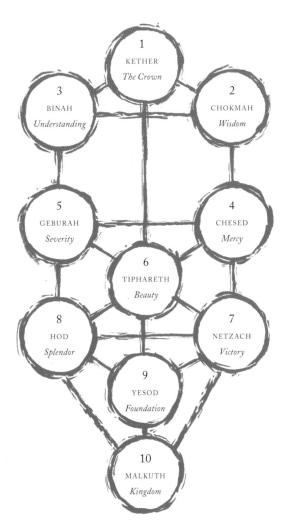

HERMETIC TAROT ·

During the course of its development, the Tarot became closely connected with the Tree of Life. The association has enriched both traditions. The Tree of Life holds a more ancient lineage, being derived from the mystical aspect of Judaism, called Qabalah. Like the Tarot, this tradition has undergone development and change. Once the Tree of Life and its teachings were exclusively the province of the Rabbis, but non-Jewish Hermetic thinkers found much in Qabalah and began to reshape it.

Imagine, if you can, a sacred philosophy of life explained entirely in pictorial form. Tibetan Buddhism approached this with its Wheel of Life, but Buddhism has never been a persecuted belief system; it did not need to hide its teachings away for safety reasons. Mystical Judaism has often been persecuted; it found a safe refuge in a pictorial representation that could not be understood by its enemies. So two complex symbol systems, the Tarot and the Tree of Life, met and meshed with each other. Like a perfect marriage, the two systems had much in common. The Tarot has 22 Major trumps; the Hebrew alphabet has 22 letters. The Tree of Life shows ten emanations individually called Sephirah; the Tarot has ten numbered cards in each suit. The Tree of Life represents the four elements of earth, air, fire, and water using four sacred letters –*Yod, He, Vau,* and a second *He*. Taken together, these letters form the most Holy Name of God. The Tarot represents the four elements as the four suits. These correspondences were noted and elaborated by both Court de Gébelin and later by Eliphas Levi, who both redefined Tarot as a spiritual art. The marriage of the Tarot and the Tree was completed by the Hermetic Order of the Golden Dawn and continued by all who still follow in these footsteps.

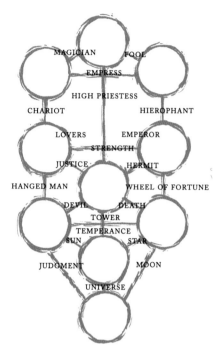

Above: The trumps of the Major Arcana are allied to the 22 paths on the Tree of Life.

The Tree of Life can be thought of as a map. The ten Sephiroth together portray unfolding creation. The first Sephirah, Kether, represents the divine source of all things. The tenth Sephirah, Malkuth, represents the final concrete outcome, the Kingdom. For those studying the Tarot, the Tree of Life provides several key principles that may be applied with good effect.

THE TREE AND THE MAJOR ARCANA

The 22 trumps of the Major Arcana are placed on the Tree of Life so they fit on its 22 paths. The path carries the usual meaning as a way of traveling from one place to another, except that the traveling takes place in the mind, through meditation upon the trump and all its related symbolism.

THE TREE AND THE MINOR ARCANA

The cards of the Minor Arcana are assigned to each of the Sephirah by number, so that the Twos fit into the second Sephirah, and so on. The divinatory significance shares in the nature of the Sephirah. Understanding this basic principle means that you do not have to attempt to learn 56 separate meanings.

If your mind delights in symbols, you will find much to treasure in the Hermetic Tarot and the Tree of Life.

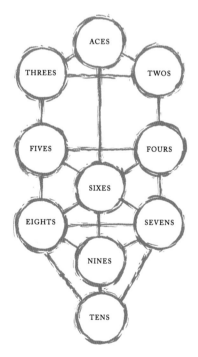

ABOVE: *The ten Sephiroth are matched by the numbers of the Minor Arcana.*

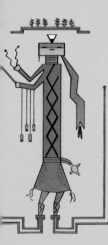

FOOL

Radical Potential

MAGICIAN HIGH PRIESTESS

Primordial Masculine/Feminine

EMPRESS EMPEROR HIEROPHANT

Conditioning *Child Environment*

LOVERS CHARIOT STRENGTH HERMIT

Skills *Education* *Training*

WHEEL OF FORTUNE

Transpersonal Perspective

JUSTICE HANGED MAN DEATH TEMPERANCE

Karmic Pattern Realized

DEVIL TOWER

Testing Blocks

STAR MOON SUN JUDGMENT

Deep Inner Work

WORLD

Transformation and Integration

The Major and Minor Arcana

THE SPIRITUAL JOURNEY

After a brief introduction to the Major and Minor Arcana, it is now time to meet them again. Although the two Arcana are quite different, they work together at all times. It is common to describe the 22 characters of the Major Arcana as stages in the journey of life, beginning with the Fool and ending with the World. This portrays our journey through life, from the innocence of childhood, to eventually establishing our place in the world.

The Fool represents individuality and our potential and innate capacity for development. The Magician and the High Priestess stand for the masculine and feminine parts of our nature. Eastern philosophy refers to these qualities as yin and yang, the active and passive poles of our capacity. The Empress, the Emperor, and the Hierophant stand for the crucial factors of the mother, the father, and an abstracted authority most often represented by a religious figurehead.

The Lovers, the Chariot, and Strength represent the skills that we acquire in social and practical areas. The Hermit represents the voice of our own wisdom that speaks as conscience and guidance as we develop. The Wheel carries us toward contact with the greater social world of events – circumstances that we cannot control. Justice, the Hanged Man, Death, and Temperance present us with highly personalized opportunities for change, growth, and development. We may choose to see these as karmic lessons from another lifetime, or as the opportunities presented by this life.

The Devil and the Tower provide the testing ground of life. These are the personal crashes and big disappointments that ask us to muster all we have to start again. The Star, the Moon, the Sun, and Judgment all represent transformative possibilities that have meaning only after life has tested us. Finally, the World represents a state of integration and acceptance of who we are as people. The journey is complete.

Earth

Air

Water

Fire

THE FOUR PATHS

If the Major Arcana describes the journey of life, the Minor Arcana describes the byways and meandering paths of daily interaction. The Minor Arcana consists of 56 cards. These are divided into four suits called Batons (also Staves, Wands, or Rods), Disks (or Coins), Cups, and Swords. The four suits are related to the four elements and other qualities of being as shown in the illustrations below.

ABOVE: *Coins are related to earth, introversion, practicality, and a lack of spirituality.*

ABOVE: *Swords are linked to air, extroversion, communication, and conflict.*

ABOVE: *Wands represent the fire element, power, energy, and destructiveness.*

ABOVE: *Cups are allied to water, sensitivity, the emotions, and selfish behavior.*

Although contemporary Tarot has provided a new set of names for the suits, the allocation to the elements remains standard. Once we have grasped the basic elemental connections, we can move on to consider how the meaning of each card is derived. The Hermetic branch assigned individual names and astrological signatures to the minor cards. These help us to categorize and sort the 56 cards into groups that are easy to remember. You will be able to decide whether you find these attributions helpful or not. We will encounter the Minor Arcana by name and astrological signature later when we meet the four elements and the suits in more depth. The Minor Arcana correspond to a deck of standard playing cards: Swords are Spades, Wands are Clubs, Cups are Hearts, and Coins are Diamonds.

0 | The Fool

VII FOOL

ABOVE: *The Fool is a mixture of trickster, jester, wise simpleton, disguised traveler, and beggar.*

THE NATURE OF THE FOOL

The Fool is a universal figure. He conceals a deep knowing that comes from standing outside the conventions of society and is often able to bring unexpected solutions to situations. The Fool displays the qualities found in children. He is playful, trusting, spontaneous, and joyful; the child who laughs at the pretensions of the adult world and shows up the absurdities and shallowness of social conventions. The Fool is a great liberator who will expose pomposity whether great and small.

Archetypal Traveler

The Fool is the archetypal traveler who stays just long enough to break old patterns and set new ones. What do you think the Fool carries? What qualities of being have been packed away ready to be unfolded? If you stand poised to take a new step in life, examine the qualities that you possess that have brought you to this point. Like the Fool, you may find that you have everything you need.

The Fool is often accompanied by an animal, commonly a dog, which is a descendant of the wilder wolf. The animal represents the instinctive life that accompanies us wherever we go.

The Fool as Soul Friend

The Fool will support you when you are faced with taking a big step or when you have lost the sense of joy in your life. The Fool is not afraid of new beginnings and sees life as a playful adventure. If you need to reconnect with the simple approach, take the Fool as your soul friend for a while. Use free movement as your meditation; dance, jump, and run with total abandon. Move with the spontaneity of a child. Put your adult training to one side for while.

Divinatory Significance

This is a time of change. Step forward with faith in the future and in yourself. Trust in the unfolding direction of your life. Move into the future with childlike simplicity. Build no great expectations either as hopes or fears. Accept what comes as it unfolds. Remain focused only on the moment.

The Fool from the Russian Tarot

Motherpeace Tarot Fool

ABOVE: *The Russian Fool is modeled on the* skomorokhi, *the traditional wandering performer who went from court to court to entertain.*

Reversed

When reversed, this trump indicates a delay or setback to plans. Perhaps you are contemplating a course of action that is not in accord with your true wishes. Look at everyone's motives in the situation. A poor choice. Look before you leap.

THE FOOL FROM THE RUSSIAN TAROT

The Fool in the Russian Tarot often carries a puppet that resembles himself, perhaps as a political comment on the lack of freedom in Russian society. He stands outside society and holds up its reflection for all to see. The ideal of the holy fool is close to the Russian spirit. It is best personified in Dostoevsky's book *The Idiot.* The Fool is Prince Myshkyn, a soul whose goodness and simplicity cause trouble to more sophisticated folks who are steeped in the ways of the world.

THE FOOL FROM THE MOTHERPEACE TAROT

The Fool is depicted as a female, attempting to cross the river by walking on her hands. She carries her possessions in a satchel balanced on one foot. The satchel is painted with an eye and adorned by a peacock feather and bells. Feathers symbolize the flight of the spirit. A lily, which represents spiritual expansion, grows in the river (symbol of life and change). A vulture (a scavenger, which attends death) oversees the adventure. The accompanying cat is attentive and involved. As a totem animal, the cat perhaps even leads the way. Magic mushrooms, with all their capacity for expansion, wait on the far bank. The crocodile serves as a warning of possible dangers involved in the crossing. The Fool is making the crossing we all must make.

Seed Thoughts

Move forward

Embrace change

Trust in life

Go with the flow

Be childlike

Key Symbols

The mountain top

The river

The journey

The seed of new beginnings

The eye of truth

I | The Magician

THE NATURE OF THE MAGICIAN

The mythology of every land is rich with tales of magic makers who shape events and weave destinies. A child's world is peopled by magical beings who have the power to change the course of events. The adult's world is, for the most part, purged of such imaginary magical beings who have been moved out to make room for more workaday companions and helpers.

A Spiritual Beginning

The figure of the Magician reminds us that magic is not just a childish delight, but an approach to the world. Every mythical wizard and shaman of every land and time is encapsulated in this figure. He or she serves to open our minds to nonphysical realities and other dimensions. The Magician welcomes us to the possibility of magical experience. This trump represents the conscious beginning of the spiritual journey, and its number is One.

The Magician as Soul Friend

The Magician will support you when you discover a deep and powerful impetus to know yourself and to claim your own natural powers. Every tradition has its own sacred path. As an entry point to the sacred life, meditate upon the ceremonial objects of the tradition to which you aspire. Treat the Magician as an elder brother who will actively share in your adventure. Perhaps the Magician will come to you in a dream as teacher, shaman, sage, wizard, or master of ceremonies.

Divinatory Significance

The Magician signifies the quest for self-realization and denotes initiative and action. This card can indicate decision-making, organization, even managerial qualities. The presence of this trump suggests the need to act positively and forcefully, to take control of a situation. This is the card of the individual who wields the baton of authority with skill on behalf of the common good.

BELOW: *The Angel of Magic from the Angels Tarot. In shamanic cultures, spiritual and magical experiences are bound together.*

1   **THE MAGICIAN**
Orangewind Yei

LEFT: *The Santa Fe
Tarot depicts the
Magician as a shaman,
a medicine man in con-
tact with the spirit world,
who practiced magic.*

Reversed

When reversed, this trump indicates hesitation,
unwillingness to act, failure to grasp an opportunity, self-serving manipulation, or acting in
an unethical fashion.

THE MAGICIAN FROM
THE SANTA FE TAROT

The Santa Fe Tarot shows us a magician in the
Navaho tradition. He is a shaman, Orangewind
Yei by name. He wears an eagle or thunderbird
headdress that links him with the sky and spiritual aspiration. His sacred implements are the
bull roarer and the crooked lightning stick.
Both ceremonial objects link him with the
heavens and the powerful forces of nature.
Feathers shoot from his feet to carry him into
the air. He walks upon the earth, but his spirit
knows how to fly. Rattles dangle from his arms.
He carries a medicine pouch indicating his call-
ing as a healer and man of the spirit.

The Magician

THE MAGICIAN FROM THE SCAPINI TAROT

It has been suggested that the figure of the Magician was derived
from the figure of the Renaissance carnival king who took part in the
procession before Lent. In early Tarot, this trump was known as The
Juggler or *Bataleur*. The Magician in the Scapini Tarot captures the fla-
vor and ornate symbolism of the Renaissance Tarot. Here we see the
Magician in a fairground setting. He stands behind a table where we see a
sword, a chalice, and three disks that are perhaps coins. A long baton rests
in the crook of his arm. Are we watching a carnival game in progress? Yet
these are also elemental symbols of the spiritual magician. Perhaps the viewer
must decide whether this is a charlatan or a sage.

Seed Thoughts

Believe in magic

Focus intent

Sharpen will

Seek yourself

LEFT: *The Magician in
the Scapini Tarot is a
Renaissance figure
linked to the color
(and perhaps artifice) of
the carnival.*

Key Symbols

The four elements

Heaven above

Earth below

*The connecting
bridge*

LEFT: *Shamans provided
a conduit to the spirit ·
world for the members of
their tribe.*

II | The High Priestess

ABOVE: *An Egyptian priestess. Antoine Court de Gébelin's theories about Tarot's link with the mysteries of ancient Egypt led him to rename the card traditionally known as the Papess, as the High Priestess.*

THE NATURE OF THE HIGH PRIESTESS

Antoine Court de Gébelin renamed this trump The High Priestess in keeping with his vision of an ancient Egyptian link with the Tarot. Until then, it had been known as The Papess. This is a curious title because there has never been a female pope. Some authorities believe that it is a reference to a legendary Pope Joan. Others have suggested that this card was based around a real person, Sister Manfreda, who was a relative of the powerful Visconti family. She was even elected pope by a small Lombard sect known as the Gugliemites of Bohemia. Her followers believed she was the incarnation of the Holy Spirit sent to inaugurate a new age. She died in Milan in 1281.

The Realm of Goddess

The priestess is an historical rather than a mythical figure, who served divinity, the temple, and the state. The office of priestess was honored in ancient cultures of the pre-Christian world. The Priestess of Demeter was accorded a privileged seat at the Olympic games. The classical author Plutarch dedicated two books to a priestess named Clea. This Tarot card can open a doorway into the realm of Goddess. Here we discover the gifts of intuition, magical timing, creative flowering, wise dreaming, prophetic knowing, deep understanding, ancient remembering, and blessed communion.

The High Priestess as Soul Friend

The High Priestess will support you when you seek to delve beyond the rational mind. She is your friend if you have an interest in psychic development, alternative healing, mediumship, meditation, or the many other approaches that honor soul and recognize intuition. In meditation, sit before the High Priestess and ask her to initiate you into the wisdom of body and soul.

Divinatory Significance

This card signifies the value of intuition and wisdom in any situation. It suggests a nonrational solution to a problem. This card stresses the importance of following personal feelings in present circumstances. Act from the highest sense of spiritual value and personal truth.

The High Priestess from the Thoth Tarot

The Marseilles Tarot Papess

Reversed

When reversed, this card suggests that both feelings and intuition are not being honored or adequately acknowledged. Perhaps there is an unwillingness to be guided by a woman's advice or by the voice of intuition. An imbalance between ethics and practice may be causing some discomfort.

THE HIGH PRIESTESS FROM THE THOTH TAROT

In this version of the Tarot, an enigmatic female figure sits mysteriously behind a veil that is suspended between her upraised hands. Here is a priestess who does not seem to be of this world. She seems to sit in another dimension beyond space and time. The daughter, priestess and the goddess have merged into one. She is crowned with the lunar disk. A bow rests across her knees. On this side of the veil we see crystalline forms and the fruits of the earth.

THE PAPESS FROM THE MARSEILLES TAROT

The Marseilles Tarot shows us a traditional image of female religious authority. It is a curious picture, bearing in mind that this office has never existed. She resembles the figure of the Pope. She is crowned by the state and wears a formal gown resembling priestly vestments. Her hair is hidden beneath a wimple in the tradition of a nun. The Papess and the Priestess represent two opposing poles of female spirituality.

ABOVE: *The High Priestess represents intuition, knowledge, common sense, dreams, and subconscious memory.*

Seed Thoughts

Offer wise counsel

Develop psychic understanding

Listen to lunar wisdom

Honor Goddess religion

Key Symbols

The moon

The waters

The priestess

The veil

The temple

III | The Empress

THE NATURE OF THE EMPRESS

All is not well in the kingdom of the Empress. Mother Nature has delivered a warning note to her family, unleashing shifting weather patterns, melting ice floes, floods, and fires. Agriculture has been revolutionized, allowing us to eat foods from all over the world throughout the year, but at what cost to the planet? Recently, there has been a return to organic and natural methods. Here the nature of the Empress is heeded.

The Living Earth

The Empress represents the bounty of the natural kingdom in every manifestation, as crystal, rock, and mineral; flower, shrub, and tree; insect, animal, and creature. This trump reminds us of our collective relationship with the earth. It asks us to look at our attitudes, needs, and demands. Is the earth just a storehouse to be endlessly ransacked for greed or profit?

The Empress as Soul Friend

The Empress will support you when you seek to live in accordance with an earth-centered philosophy. Take a new approach to interacting with others and nature. You can connect with the energy of the Empress as great mother by spending time outdoors – walking, gardening, resting, watching the night sky, seeing the dawn come up, becoming attuned to the seasons, planting, tending, caring, being with animals, mothering, constructing a sanctuary. Let these activities become your meditation.

ABOVE: *The symbol of the Roman goddess Venus, one of whose responsibilities was grain and crops.*

BELOW: *The Empress symbolizes the fruitful nature of earth. She enshrines respect for the natural world and its resources.*

The Motherpeace Tarot Empress

The Empress from the Russian Tarot

Divinatory Significance

The Empress signifies the renewing cycle of Nature. The card suggests fertility, possibly even a pregnancy, and creativity. This is a good time to put your energies into a creative direction. The Empress indicates a feminine force at work. There may be connections with other women or with the issues affecting women.

Reversed

When reversed, this card means something is blocking your creativity. Does it come from outside or from within yourself? Do you feel that you lack confidence in your own dreams? Try to discover where the blockage lies.

THE EMPRESS FROM THE MOTHERPEACE TAROT

The Motherpeace Tarot shows the Empress as Mother Nature. In the foreground is Demeter, the Greek mother goddess. The worship of Demeter belonged to women. During her annual festival, women marked the cycle of fertility. To the left of the Empress is a depiction of a throned figure from the ancient Turkish city of Çatal Hüyük, where the goddess was venerated. To the right is a famous statue, the Venus of Laussel, one of the oldest depictions of the Great Mother in existence.

THE EMPRESS FROM THE RUSSIAN TAROT

Individual women have, of course, held the office of Empress. The Russian Tarot shows Zoe Paleologus, who became the second wife of Ivan III in 1472. As the niece of Emperor Constantine, Zoe inherited the right to the Byzantine double eagle, which became the crest of the Czars until 1917. She was well-educated and spoke several languages. Her upbringing in exotic Constantinople gave her a love of art, which she applied to the renovation of the Moscow Kremlin. We see her seated on a throne wearing a short jacket known by the Russians as a "soul warmer."

Seed Thoughts

Plant at the right time

Cherish the earth

Steward the planet

Celebrate the harvest

Key Symbols

Venus

The great mother

The harvest

Demeter

IV | The Emperor

THE NATURE OF THE EMPEROR

History has shown us many emperors. Some have ruled wisely and well. Others have been tyrants, profligate monsters, and power-hungry autocrats. Kings, potentates, pharaohs, sultans, and czars, all have shared in the nature of the emperor, which is to rule. Absolute authority, unrestrained action, and total power has been the undoing of many. Modern-day power struggles now take place in the debating chamber, the political backroom, the board-room, the office, and the corporate structure. Wherever power resides, however great or small, so the energy of the Emperor will be found. The Emperor is present in all authority figures and in all decision-makers.

Rule Wisely and Well

Rulership means taking decisions. Every decision, like a crossroads, has the power to shape destiny, change direction, or alter course. The Emperor represents the power to rule your own life. You cannot avoid decision-making, allocating resources of time and energy, making choices, planning and organizing your time. The Emperor affirms that you are your own seat of authority. You are able to take responsibility for your own choices and actions.

BELOW: *The Houses of Parliament, seat of government in Britain. The Emperor, representing authority figures and decision-makers, will be walking these corridors!*

The Emperor as Soul Friend

The Emperor will support you when you need to organize, structure, and administer something in your life. The Emperor is a particularly good ally in the workplace when you need to be in authority, hold boundaries, and achieve specific goals. He brings logical thought processes that serve goal-oriented situations extremely well. In meditation, sit upon the throne of your life and survey the kingdom of your being.

The Emperor from the Egyptian Tarot

The Zolar Tarot's Emperor card

Divinatory Significance

This card signifies the successful organization of a project or undertaking. It may also signify the involvement of a male figure such as a boss, father, or husband. Or it may simply indicate that clear thinking, careful planning, and good organization have brought success and reward.

Reversed

When reversed, this card signifies that the kingdom is not in good order. It denotes that a person is not making balanced decisions or wielding authority wisely and well.

THE EMPEROR FROM THE EGYPTIAN TAROT

The Egyptian Tarot shows us another ancient ruler, the pharaoh. The office of pharaoh was always intended to be both leader and servant of the people. This trump is called The Cubic Stone. The cube represents stability as it is composed of six squares, each facing a different direction. Stability is to be found above and below, forward and behind, to the left and to the right.

THE EMPEROR FROM THE ZOLAR TAROT

The Zolar Tarot shows us a picture of kingship. An aged king sits on a throne carved from stone. It supports four ram-headed figures, which remind us that this trump is assigned to the sign of Aries. Aries brings the surging power of spring, coupled with the burning energy of fire. It is a sign of activity, energy, and determination. This king bears all the trappings of state and reminds us that societies have been organized around a ruling figure for both good and ill. Power so easily corrupts even the highest of ideals.

Seed Thoughts

Take charge

Be in command

Be organized

Rule from within

Key Symbols

The regalia of rulership

The throne

The ruler of the kingdom

V | The Hierophant

THE NATURE OF THE HIEROPHANT

We feel the impact of Court de Gébelin's vision when we look at this trump. The Hierophant was originally called the Pope, and was the counterpart of card II, the Papess or High Priestess. In this form it represented a traditional religious leader and a conservative approach to spiritual matters. However, when the name changed, our perspective changed, too. The title of Hierophant is unusual. It means the Revealer of Secret Things. At the ancient Greek mysteries (the religious festivities of the goddess Demeter) in the town of Eleusis, the presiding high priest was known as the hierophant. The purpose of these ceremonies was to awaken the individual to an understanding of life's value. Teaching or dogma was never a part of this; everything revolved around personal experience.

The Two Doors

The Hierophant reminds us that every religion has two faces that we call the exoteric and the esoteric. The exoteric path stresses personal behavior, dogma, traditional creed, and stated belief. The esoteric path stresses personal awakening, spiritual practice, and experience. It may come as a surprise to discover that even the monolithic traditions have an esoteric face. The Sufi path represents the inner way within Islam. Buddhism has a rich mystical heritage. Christianity has its mystical side, too, in the monastic life and devotional practices. This trump show us that the exoteric and esoteric faces of religion are to be found in the same place, one invisibly within the other. The seeker alone decides whether to rest at the outer door or continue further toward direct spiritual experience.

The Hierophant as Soul Friend

The Hierophant will support you when you are moved to ask deep questions of religion. This quest for spiritual awakening begins with questions such as, "Who am I?" "What is my purpose?" You may feel comforted by a traditional response, or you may feel the need to probe further and seek your own answers. Meditate on what you need to know. It is often said that when the pupil is ready, the teacher will appear.

LEFT: *In ancient Greece, the hierophant was a priest who presided over religious ceremonies.*

Divinatory Significance

This trump signifies that you are looking for advice from a traditional source. You have a natural respect for authority figures because you expect to receive a well-founded answer from such a expert. Perhaps you are seeking to become part of a conservative organization or set-up as you find safety in the tried and tested way.

Reversed

When reversed, this trump indicates a willingness to seek answers from a nontraditional or even unusual teaching figure who expresses a natural authority and wisdom. You feel comfortable with the new.

THE HIEROPHANT FROM THE GOLDEN DAWN TAROT

The Order of the Golden Dawn created new ceremonies that were built on the models left by the ancient world. They attempted to revitalize ancient wisdom, not merely by study, but by involvement and participation. So although this trump shows us another priestly figure on a throne, looking quite traditional, the Golden Dawn were in fact highly unorthodox in their interpretation. This is an image of a hierophant as the Revealer of Secret Things, and not a purveyor of handed-down words. He is an influential teacher.

THE HIEROPHANT FROM THE MARSEILLES TAROT

In the Marseilles Tarot, we see a traditional and conservative picture of religious authority. Two figures stand before the papal figure, who dispenses a blessing. Many choose to follow leaders who present the teachings of the tradition. Organized religions call on the support of millions of people around the world.

Golden Dawn Tarot Hierophant

Marseilles Tarot Pope

Seed Thoughts

Seek the teacher

Hear advice

Where is Holiness?

Quest diligently

Key Symbols

Religious authority

The Church

The Temple

The Holy Place

VI | The Lovers

THE NATURE OF THE LOVERS

Every nation has its own stories of great love between two people. It does not matter whether such stories are fact or fiction. We are moved by tales of passionate involvement and commitment. Great love stories endure the test of time. Shakespeare's *Romeo and Juliet* grips every generation by its portrayal of tragic young love. Such is the nature of love that it defies obstacles and overcomes everything put in its path. The desire for union is overwhelming. Our need to be loved is inborn. Our search for the beloved has no end. The urge to express love is universal and timeless, itself an extraordinary and wonderful human quality.

Falling in love is often inexplicable. Who can explain the mutual attraction that arises between two people? Mischievous Cupid randomly fires darts of love and desire, reminding us that love can arise quite unexpectedly. It is often said that opposites attract: yin and yang come together to make a whole.

Joining Together

Who does not want to give love and be loved in return? All relationships are built on this. Love seems to be the simplest and most natural expression of the heart. The rose has long been the flower of love. Its beauty and its thorns remind us of the mixed blessing when we open ourselves to love.

The Lovers as Soul Friend

This trump will support you when you seek the companionship and friendship of a partner. It reminds you of what can be gained when two people come together in trust. Open your heart to the infinite possibility of love. Meditate on what you can give and receive as lover and the beloved.

Divinatory Significance

This trump indicates that a choice is being offered, but you need to know what you want in order to choose correctly. Be sure you understand what is being offered. This card stresses the positive nature of a relationship in your life and suggests the significance of an honest and loving partnership.

LEFT: *This blindfolded Cupid, from the Marseilles Tarot, ensures that his arrows are fired randomly!*

Reversed

When reversed, this card indicates that you feel uncertain about what you want for yourself. Any forthcoming decisions are colored by your lack of clarity and direction. The advice of others just adds to your confusion.

THE LOVERS FROM THE SCAPINI TAROT

This trump shows us a traditional picture of two lovers holding hands. They are richly dressed, indicating that the two families have a vested interest in the success of this marriage. In the distance behind the figures is a castle, perhaps representing the worldly goods that each brings to the union. Hovering above the pair is the blindfolded figure of Cupid. He aims the arrow of love at the woman's heart. Will this pair find happiness? Love is indeed blind!

THE LOVERS FROM THE SANTA FE TAROT

The Santa Fe Tarot shows us unusual representations of the Lovers as White Corn Man and Yellow Corn Woman. These are called Two-who-follow-one-another. Their mating resulted in the birth of the Corn People. Yellow Corn Woman and White Corn Man are forever linked by the corn beetle, which scurries from one to the other.

Seed Thoughts

Value the other

Love yourself

Honor the beloved

Key Symbols

Yin and yang

Opposites

Polarity

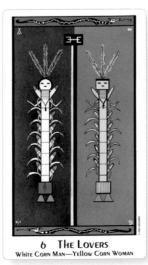

FAR LEFT: *The Lovers of the Scapini Tarot are dressed in rich apparel to indicate that they are both high born.*

LEFT: *The Santa Fe Tarot Lovers are the distinctive White Corn Man and Yellow Corn Woman.*

VII | The Chariot

ABOVE: *The figure of the charioteer shows us self-mastery, guiding the chariot without any visible signs. All control has become internalized.*

THE NATURE OF THE CHARIOT

The chariot belongs to history. By comparison, its modern counterpart, the car, provides only a faint echo of excitement. The modern vehicle runs on invisible horsepower. The chariot of old was driven by the power of horses. Imagine that you are given the reins to guide two headstrong, independent, and powerful animals. How would you achieve control? What would happen if you could not blend the independent energies of the creatures at your disposal? Do you have all that is required to control, direct, and harmonize the powers at the disposal of the charioteer?

Moving Forward Through Life

This trump gives us three aspects of life to explore: the chariot, the charioteer, and the motive power driving the chariot. The Chariot is an expression of a life set against a cosmic background. Its starry sky and four pillars encompass the world. The charioteer portrays consciousness, the ability to choose direction and set a course. The beasts, whether horses or sphinxes, represent the drives, motivations, and passions that we experience: our commitment, stamina, dedication, or focused intent as we set a course in life.

As the seventh trump, the Chariot is often thought to complete the cycle begun with the step of the Fool. The elemental symbols laid out by the magician have become internalized within the psyche. The intention expressed by the Magician has been translated into a completely unified philosophy of living and being. Chariot, charioteer, and driving powers move forward as one, with known direction, clear purpose, and pure intent.

The Chariot as Soul Friend

The Chariot will support you in establishing control of your life. The charioteer represents your ability to harmonize the competing forces that we all have to balance in our lives. Balancing the competing demands of home and work, career and family, self and others is no easy task. It requires constant adjustment and rebalancing. In meditation, see yourself as the charioteer and allocate each of the passions and demands in your life to the driving beasts. Discover how these powers harmonize with or oppose one another.

LEFT: The film Ben Hur *contains classic images of the power of the charioteer and his thundering horses.*

Divinatory Significance

This card signifies mastery, equilibrium, and success. Reason and emotion now work together; intellect and intuition support each other in a common direction. You have many talents and abilities to draw on in an undertaking.

The Thoth deck Charioteer

Reversed

When reversed, this card indicates a loss of control, defeat, and vacillation. Your direction is unclear. An imbalance threatens to upset the outcome.

THE CHARIOT FROM THE THOTH TAROT

The charioteer in the Thoth Tarot is called Lord of the Triumph of Light. He stands as a grail knight armored in gold. He shows the grail to you. His chariot is drawn by the elemental beasts. Here are the competing forces of mind, body, heart, and spirit in peaceful harmony and cooperation. The elemental symbols once set upon the Magician's table have become the driving components of the charioteer's victory. This charioteer drives without reins. His chariot extends between the heights and the depths. It is life itself.

The Charioteer of the Marseilles Tarot

THE CHARIOT FROM THE MARSEILLES TAROT

The charioteer from the Marseilles Tarot stands somewhere between the warrior of history and the knight of legend. He is a crowned prince enjoying fruits that were perhaps won by others, revelling in a sense of victory and achievement. The medieval chariot has become a showpiece of state power rather than a challenge of the battlefield or the race arena. The Cart of the Marseilles Tarot lacks the quality of dynamism and vitality found in contemporary Tarot.

Seed Thoughts

Mastery through balance

Direction through consciousness

Control through skill

Key Symbols

The chariot

The driver

The beasts

VIII | Strength

THE NATURE OF STRENGTH

This trump depicts an unequal battle between a woman and a lion. Yet victory lies with the woman. She triumphs through spiritual strength. She overcomes her adversary, who has a far superior physical strength. Here is a theme we can all recognize from life and from history. David beat Goliath in a battle of unequal force. The simple Gandhi brought down the great empire of the British in India. Aung San Su Kyi stands against the Burmese government. Nelson Mandela emerged victorious after years of imprisonment. Such conditions would have destroyed the morale of a lesser person.

Defeating the Enemy

The adversary takes many forms: as political oppressor, corporate body, intimidating manager, playground bully, social restriction, and physical illness. This enemy has many faces. Here are all the obstacles that block our way in life and all the experiences that intimidate and threaten to reduce us. This trump shows us that victory is possible. Strength is invariably depicted by a woman to show that the feminine qualities have the power to turn an

enemy into a friend. This kind of strength comes from within through love, compassion, and self-knowledge.

Strength as Soul Friend

Strength will support you when you need an inner ally in a battle that seems unequal. The enemy may seem all-powerful, and you may feel weak and intimidated, yet you know you have moral right on your side. Meditate on the figure of Strength when you need to be supported in your course of action.

Strength from the Motherpeace Tarot

The Egyptian Tarot card for Strength

Divinatory Significance

This card shows you that your valuable qualities of self-knowledge and compassionate love have the power to affect others in a beneficial way. Spiritual strength empowers. A victory is possible. Don't be dragged down to the same level as your opponent. A positive card, but make sure that you keep yourself focused.

Reversed

When reversed, this card indicates a situation where your strength is only superficial. It represents a weakness or uncertainty disguised as bravado. Don't abuse the power that you have at your disposal.

STRENGTH FROM THE MOTHERPEACE TAROT

The Motherpeace trump shows us the Irish goddess Brigid surrounded by 12 animals. She is safe in this company even though some of these animals are powerful and dangerous. She has developed a great inner strength by coming to understand herself as part of creation.

STRENGTH FROM THE EGYPTIAN TAROT

This trump is called the Tamed Lion. A woman in Egyptian robes holds open the mouth of lion. The lion represents a powerful force that has been tamed. It might even represent something within, such as anger or greed. Powerful instincts have often been shown in art and literature as demons or threatening beasts. The woman wears a serpent crown, showing she has a highly developed spiritual understanding.

Seed Thoughts

Triumphant spirit

Face the enemy

Find courage

Key Symbols

The animal nature

The spiritual nature

IX | The Hermit

ABOVE: *The Zolar Tarot Hermit. This character symbolizes independence, wisdom, and self-knowledge.*

THE NATURE OF THE HERMIT

The hermit life is rare these days. Buddhism favors long periods of solitary retreat, but outside a spiritual life such solitude is not the norm. Solitary confinement is a form of torture designed to push a person to the absolute limit. The absence of the warmth of others is a desperate deprivation. Yet the hermit and the monk on long retreat choose the solitude of personal silence in order to discover the absolute limits of being. Every spiritual tradition has produced its hermits, lone travelers who have spent long years in a life of continuous meditation and contemplation, but this is a path that few choose to pursue.

Clarity of Mind

The hermit treads a path that others may follow if they wish. The lamp of truth shines out for others who also walk the spiritual path. Intense isolation can bring clarity of mind, inner vision, and sense of purpose. The incubation chamber of soulful prayer and meditation can act as midwife to spiritual creativity. The inspired works that arise serve as a beacon of light to others.

As life continues to become increasingly hectic and demanding, the space offered by spiritual retreat, no matter how brief, is becoming increasingly appealing. Monastic institutions are prepared to open their doors to guests. Others take to a wilderness retreat. Such interludes away from work and home provide breathing spaces for the spirit and the whole person. There is much to be gained from this withdrawal. It is a faint echo of the hermit life.

The Hermit as Soul Friend

The Hermit will support you when you seek to withdraw from everyday life, even for a short while, as a way of finding peace. Being alone with your own thoughts is probably a new experience. We are not used to silence or to such a dramatic change of routine. Try a short period of continuous meditation, perhaps just an afternoon, to get a glimpse of the hermit's way of life.

Divinatory Significance

This trump indicates that you tread a spiritual path in life. Although this may have led you into periods of loneliness, it has given you the strength of

LEFT: *The Hermit's lamp represents the insights that come from meditation to inspire creativity.*

your own convictions. You are also open to advice from others on the path, whom you see as mentor figures. Generally, this trump represents advice from a reliable source.

Reversed

When reversed, this card means that you are not listening to any advice. You do not have the confidence to heed the guidance of your own inclinations and you are not open enough to hear what others are saying.

THE HERMIT FROM THE EGYPTIAN TAROT

In the Egyptian Tarot, this trump is called the Veiled Lamp. The name shifts our attention from the individual to the lamp itself. The veiled lamp signifies the eternal light of truth and wisdom. Spiritual truth is often represented by a light in the darkness. It is represented in the church or temple by a sacred flame. The light of truth shines out for every generation.

THE HERMIT FROM THE SCAPINI TAROT

This hermit stands like a giant towering above the landscape. He resembles a Chinese sage with flowing oriental robes and long white beard. His massive stature stands for the wisdom tradition that stretches across every land. He carries a lamp and a staff with roses entwined and a serpent in the shape of a caduceus. The caduceus is a sign of healing and medicine.

The Egyptian Tarot Hermit card)

The Scapini Tarot Hermit

Seed Thoughts

Retreat within

Enter solitude

Find yourself

Key Symbols

The wise traveler

The lamp of truth

The journey

10 Wheel of Fortune
Winding, Rainbow

X | The Wheel

ABOVE: *The Zolar Wheel, a card that signifies change, the swing of fortunes from good to bad, then back again – all wheels must turn full circle.*

THE NATURE OF THE WHEEL

The wheel is a common image for many cultures. It signifies the repeating cycles of time that arise from the movement of the earth. Day and night occur as the earth spins. The seasons change as the earth moves in its orbit. The seasonal cycle of the year is often likened to a turning wheel, and ancient calendars were often circular. When the year is seen as a wheel it becomes natural to celebrate the turning points at the solstices and equinoxes. A circle has no beginning and no end. The Wheel expresses time without end. Life changes continuously as we move through time. The only permanence is impermanence. The constantly turning wheel is a perfect expression of this.

Everything Changes

Buddhism in particular recognizes the importance of understanding change. Remembering impermanence reminds us not to cling too tightly to any particular experience – it will pass, and life will move on. The Wheel of Life is painted in Buddhist monasteries to show the cycles of life and death. Buddhism teaches reincarnation, which again lends itself to the symbolism of the wheel. The Medicine Wheel of Native American spirituality also expresses a living philosophy. This trump has also been called the Wheel of Fortune. A meteoric rise to fame and fortune can be followed by the crash of expectations. The wheel is constantly turning.

ABOVE: *All the Native American tribes have medicine wheels, whose functions include helping the individual to find inner peace.*

The Wheel as Soul Friend

The Wheel will support you when you feel that your life has become stagnant. It may appear that nothing is changing for you at a particular moment, but the wheel of life turns without ceasing. Meditate on change and impermanence. The wheel will turn again.

Divinatory Significance

The Wheel reveals a run of good luck. A rewarding period when everything seems to flow well. An advantageous turn of events. You are blessed with perfect timing. Fortune is smiling on you.

Motherpeace Wheel

Reversed

When reversed, this card indicates an unexpected turn of events: delays, hindrances, recurring problems and setbacks, complications you did not foresee. You might feel as though you are hitting an invisible brick wall.

THE WHEEL FROM THE MOTHERPEACE TAROT

The circular shape of the Motherpeace Tarot Wheel card suits this trump perfectly. This Wheel card takes the astrological cycle of the year as its theme. It shows us the planetary system surrounded by the twelve signs of the zodiac. These are depicted using various goddess images from different times and places. This trump reminds us that the cycles of our lives are connected to the greater wheel of the heavens. Astrology seeks to show us how the cosmic patterns are reflected in our lives.

Zolar Wheel

Seed Thoughts

Nothing lasts

Everything changes

Impermanence is permanent

Key Symbols

The wheel

Fortune

THE WHEEL FROM THE ZOLAR TAROT

In the center of this card is a wheel that is divided by eight spokes. It carries the letters that spell the word *rota,* meaning wheel, *tora,* meaning the law, and of course *taro.* A strange creature signifying the forces of evolution turns with the wheel. In each of the corners are the elemental signs for earth, air, fire and water. This reminds us that creation draws upon these four powers as it turns through time. A sphinx sits with a sword, perhaps ready to release everyone from the wheel.

XI | Justice

THE NATURE OF JUSTICE

The concept of justice is ancient. It is also a very sophisticated idea that recognizes that all behavior has consequences. The first written law code appeared with the Babylonians. Justice and law are connected – there cannot be one without the other. The figure of Justice holds the scales in one hand and the sword in the other. The law exists to uphold justice. The depictions of justice in the Tarot invariably include the scales, which represent Libra, the sign of harmony and balance. The figure of Justice that stands above the Old Bailey law courts in London today still holds the scales. She is blindfolded to show her impartiality. It is difficult to imagine a society without a concept of justice. Although this trump clearly carries legal implications, it also relates to the law of karma, which works unseen through the unfolding events of life: the way you behave in life affects your existence after death.

Weighing the Heart

The Egyptians had very subtle ideas about morality and the effects of behavior. They believed that the seat of human conscience lay in the heart. The heart contained all the deeds, actions, and intentions of a lifetime. Upon death the soul had to face the judgment hall and stand answerable for a life. In the judgment hall, the heart was weighed against the feather of truth that belonged to Maat, the goddess of truth and right order.

Justice as Soul Friend

Justice will support you when you need to see the justice of a situation. If your need for justice is tangible enough, you may feel moved to have recourse to law. More often, you will just want to understand the competing claims in a situation. In meditation, place your concerns in the scales of justice and be open to the outcome.

LEFT: *The figure of Justice usually carries a sword, indicating that justice is worth fighting for.*

Divinatory Significance

This trump indicates receiving what is deserved, the rightful distribution of proceeds, praise and blame, the rightful portion, and actions taking place that bring a better balance to life. This trump might indicate hard lessons to learn in life that show that karmic factors are operating.

Reversed

When reversed, this trump indicates unfairness, or not reaching an equitable solution. You might feel as if your rights have been violated – a poor judgment perhaps, or even a prejudiced decision. Success in legal proceedings is unlikely.

Justice from the Motherpeace Tarot

JUSTICE FROM THE MOTHERPEACE TAROT

Here we see the three Norse goddesses of destiny who congregate at the ash tree. They pause to deliberate: one goddess waters the tree; a second sits with her hand against the root, taking its life pulse; the third reaches out to a deer. The Motherpeace is a broader view of justice, which takes the whole of life into account. The presence of these three goddesses indicates that justice is done in our lives through personal destiny, fate, and circumstance.

The Thoth Tarot Justice

JUSTICE FROM THE THOTH TAROT

The trump in the Thoth Tarot is called Adjustment. Justice is included in the wider concept of karmic balancing. Occultist Aleister Crowley presents us with an awesome figure. She is crowned with the ostrich feathers of Maat, the Egyptian goddess of truth. She and the scales are almost as one. She is masked and holds a sword, its point resting on the ground while our fate is decided. We see the Greek signs, alpha and omega, indicating the beginning and end of any situation.

Seed Thoughts

Weigh the heart

Balance the scales

Acknowledge karma

Key Symbols

The scales

The sword

The blindfold

XII | The Hanged Man

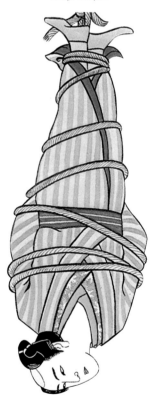

THE NATURE OF THE HANGED MAN

This trump presents us with a distinctly unusual image. Hanging upside down is outside the range of normal activity. It is designed to make us stop and think. What is happening here? How has this young man come to be hung upside down? This does not look like a punishment. Indian holy men are famous for undertaking extreme and unusual physical feats as a way of proving mastery of mind and spirit. Children take delight in walking on their hands, or simply enjoy looking at the world from an upside-down point of view. When you take an upside-down view of the world, you gain a new perspective, perhaps becoming more adaptable.

The Price of Knowledge

The tree is an important image in mythology: it represents the source of knowledge or wisdom. The tree is rooted in the earth, and its branches reach out to the heavens. It stands like a living bridge between the knowledge of the heavens and the knowledge of the earth. To hang from the tree in a passive state is to surrender to the tree of knowledge. Odin, the Norse god of wisdom, hung on the tree for nine days. Buddha sat beneath the Bodhi tree, where he found enlightenment. This trump tells us that knowledge and wisdom are achieved through taking a reversed position. We will have to suspend the activities of normal life for a while in order to do this.

The Hanged Man as Soul Friend

This trump will support you when you recognize that your value system has shifted so deeply that you feel different. You might even be losing friends who no longer share your interests. However, your new perspective gives you a wider view, and you would not return to a more orthodox position now.

Divinatory Significance

You are looking at the world differently – taking a new look at life, getting a new perspective on yourself perhaps. As a result, old ideas are falling away. You have gained more understanding of both past and future. Your new perspective may ask sacrifices of you so that you can focus on what is important.

Reversed

When reversed, this card signifies that you may have hang-ups that are holding you back. Is a new position so hard to adopt? Stand your value system on its head, and what do you see?

THE HANGED MAN FROM THE SANTA FE TAROT

The hanged man is called Blue Whirlwind boy. His story is told in the journey for knowledge and power. Blue Whirlwind boy is the son of Black Wind. Blue Whirlwind boy was rash and ignored his father's instructions. He was kidnapped first by the Thunder and then by the Cyclone people. He escaped and hid in a hole in a rock. Eventually, he was restored to his family. The card shows him in hiding. Trapped suns serve as his rattle. Life stands in suspension.

THE HANGED MAN FROM THE ZOLAR TAROT

A young man hangs suspended by a single foot from a tree in the shape of a T. Light radiates from his head, and he appears to be in no discomfort. The tree reminds us of the tree of knowledge.

Seed Thoughts

Look again

Find a new perspective

Stand everything on its head

12 THE HANGED MAN
Blue Whirlwind Boy

FAR LEFT: *In the Santa Fe Tarot, the man is Blue Whirlwind boy, who achieves wisdom after a frightening adventure. Here he is hiding.*

LEFT: *The Zolar Hanged Man is lashed to a tree, alluding to the tree of knowledge of good and evil described in the Book of Genesis.*

Key Symbols

The Tree of Knowledge

XIII | Death

ABOVE: *The mystical view of death as a transition through a tunnel of light has now been supported by many "near-death" experiences.*

ABOVE RIGHT: *Death is also depicted as a knight on horseback.*

THE NATURE OF DEATH

Death is perhaps the only certainty of life. Death has often been characterized by the grim reaper cutting down the harvest or the pale rider on a white horse. He has also been described as a ferryman, but rarely has Death ever been cast in anything other than a grim disguise. This card is numbered 13, the traditionally unlucky number. Death is something we do not want to think about. In the West people have almost succeeded in making death invisible. Death has become removed from everyday life, yet it remains one of its few certainties.

The Tunnel of Light

Spiritual traditions have always taught that death is a passage to a different mode of life. Those who believe in reincarnation also believe that we have died on many occasions. Every spiritual tradition urges us to prepare for death through meditation. Buddhism asks that we remind ourselves of the inevitability of our own passing. It reminds us to live mindfully as we have no way of knowing when death will come. Buddhism offers meditative practices to prepare for the state in between lives.

The appearance of this card is traditionally feared in a spread, but it does not have to signify a physical death. More often it reminds us that life is changing and that a cycle of experiences is coming to a close.

Death as Soul Friend

It is perhaps impossible to think of Death as a soul friend, but remember that your body undergoes a continuous process of death and rebirth through cell and tissue renewal. Death is a certainty. Are you able to meditate on the inevitability of your own death?

Divinatory Significance

A positive card indicating a brand new way of life, new opportunities, and new possibilities. A stage in your life is coming to an end. When this is complete, a new cycle can begin. Your life is being transformed.

ABOVE: *The heraldic rose from the flag carried by the horseman Death on the Zolar Tarot card seen top left.*

RIGHT: *Death often carries a scythe to reap a crop of the living, earning the name of "grim reaper."*

Reversed

When reversed, this card means that life feels as if it has come to a standstill. There is a sense of stagnation and procrastination. You feel as if you are waiting for something to happen. Your life feels becalmed. This, too, will pass.

DEATH FROM THE GOLDEN DAWN TAROT

As we might expect from the Tarot of a metaphysical group, we are given a different perspective. Death in the form of the skeleton is here once more. He even reduces kings with his scythe. But in the sky we see the eagle and the serpent as powerful images of renewing life. The high-flying eagle represents spiritual freedom. The serpent, which grows by shedding its skin, symbolizes renewal. Although we see death here, we are also shown the symbols of a transformative process.

DEATH FROM THE RUSSIAN TAROT

Here we see a death on the battlefield. The landscape is barren. We see the discarded weapons of war: a quiver of arrows, abandoned shields and swords, a decomposing head. Russia has, of course, witnessed terrible scenes of combat and destruction. Thousands have died on her soil. This card seems to point out the folly and futility of war. War brings self-inflicted death.

Seed Thoughts

Life continues

Live fully in the moment

Transformation is continuous

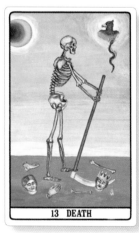

LEFT: *The Russian Tarot version of Death refers to the horror of the battles that have punctuated Russia's history.*

FAR LEFT: *The Golden Dawn card for Death. Kings and commoners are shown to be equally vulnerable to the sweep of Death's scythe.*

Key Symbols

The River Styx

The ferryman

The reaper

XIV | Temperance

THE NATURE OF TEMPERANCE

This card shows the figure of an angel. In the Tarot, angelic figures represent a higher consciousness. Temperance as a balancing force pours liquid from one vessel to another until the two become blended into a new solution. It seems perfect that the word "solution" describes both a liquid in which a substance has been dissolved, and is also to be found in the term "resolution" in which a problem has been dissolved. A good solution is not a matter of giving in, but of truly finding a way forward that includes the needs of both parties. Temperance is in the act of creating a new solution.

Finding the Middle Way

Temperance describes the middle way – extreme positions always lead to a polarization and make compromise very hard to find. As we acknowledge another viewpoint, we are changed. As a result we, too, are tempered. All negotiated settlements and peace treaties find the way forward through a tempered solution. Compromise is important in all walks of life and in all aspects of it, from the political to the personal.

ABOVE: *The Temperance angel pours liquid from one pitcher to another. The card symbolizes moderation in all things.*

Temperance as Soul Friend

Temperance will support you when you are faced with two opposing claims and searching for a middle way that satisfies both. Temperance represents a creative solution to your dilemma. In meditation, pour both sides of the problem into two containers and turn them back and forth over and over again. When they have become blended, a new solution may arise.

Divinatory Significance

This trump signifies moderation and a creative solution to a problem that involves two different factors. Put your beliefs into practice – seek equilibrium and cooperation. Meet others halfway and find the middle road.

Reversed

When reversed, this card suggests the inability to find a balance point. You lack self-control. You cannot make up your mind. You keep making the same mistakes. You cannot see the way to harmonize the many competing interests. But taking an extreme stance will not take you forward. Look again for a negotiated settlement.

TEMPERANCE FROM THE SCAPINI TAROT

We see a winged figure balanced rather precariously upon different-shaped blocks. One arm is raised high to pour liquid from a silver ewer shaped like the moon into a golden pitcher shaped like a lion. The two vessels represent the opposite forces in our nature. In Eastern metaphysics, these are often called yin and yang. In the West these same qualities are shown as the sun and moon, or as gold and silver. Temperance, the balancing power, pours from one to the other. In the foreground we see Christ's baptism scene. Perhaps the balance of opposing forces brings a baptism into the spiritual life.

TEMPERANCE FROM THE THOTH TAROT

In this Tarot, the trump is called Art as a reference to alchemy – sometimes called the secret art. Crowley has replaced the older image with a very unusual idea drawn from the tradition of alchemy. Its stated aim of turning base metal into gold is a metaphor for elevating ordinary human qualities into their highest form. The angel figure is composed of two opposite parts, one dark, one light. The eagle and lion are alchemical beasts. The cauldron represents the psyche. It is heated from beneath by a furnace. Great change is taking place as fire and water are combined. A stream of light rises to form two rainbows, which settle like a cape around the angelic figure. This is a card of living transformation.

Thoth Tarot Temperance

Temperance from the Scapini Tarot

Seed Thoughts

Undergo change

Balance the opposite

Seek resolution

Find a middle way

Key Symbols

The chemical vessel

Dark and light

XV | The Devil

ABOVE: *The Devil is traditionally represented in different ways. Here he appears as a goat in a 17th-century painting entitled "A Diablerie."*

THE NATURE OF THE DEVIL

The Devil is depicted in animal form, often as a combination of animals. As the powerful lion represents obstacles in life, so the traditional form of the Devil shows us how we can become trapped by these obstacles. Many of the Tarot cards depict a man and a woman chained to a devilish being. We need to ask ourselves how we are chained to a devil of our own making.

Greed Makes Us Ugly

This trump is related to our view of the world and its resources. Native and nomadic peoples have never sought to own the resources at their disposal. The Devil is depicted as a distorted human. Desire for possessions can distort the way people treat each other. Greed makes us monstrous. This card is attributed to Capricorn, a sign that represents earthly qualities. It was once believed that everything earthly was fallen and corrupted, and only the things of heaven and the spirit were pure and good. This idea has lasted a long time. It seems sad that our beautiful world should be thought impure.

The Devil as Soul Friend

This may seem like a contradiction in terms. Traditionally, the Devil has been a figure of temptation, but this is not how the Tarot sees him. When you have befriended your fears and limitations, you will be free to take off the chains that have held you back. Think about your relationship to your possessions. How much time and energy do you expend on what you own?

Divinatory Significance

This trump indicates that you have become caught up in a situation that brings little joy. Yet the way out lies in your own hands, though you are unable to see it. You feel trapped and miserable. What has enslaved you – another person, your own fears, money, your career?

Reversed

When reversed, this trump indicates a sense of liberation as a problem disappears. Lessons concerning greed or possessiveness have been learned.

LEFT: *The Devil as a fearsome, fire-breathing dragon, with wings echoing his former angelic status.*

THE DEVIL FROM THE GOLDEN THE TAROT

This Tarot presents a very traditional image of the Devil. A towering figure stands upon a cubic stone to which a man and a woman are chained. It is the same cubic stone as that of the Egyptian Tarot in trump IV, the Emperor. Whereas the Emperor represents rulership in earthly matters, the Devil represents the abuse and misunderstanding of worldly possessions. The scene is dark and gloomy. There is no light in the life of these people who have become chained to their goods. Yet they are only loosely chained at the wrist and so could easily walk away from this way of life.

THE DEVIL FROM THE SANTA FE TAROT

The monster here is called Sand Dune monster. He is both a mythical being and a fact of life for people living near the desert. His feet are square and contain small circles indicating that he wishes to hold the world in his grip. Imagine a town engulfed by sand. Sand has the power to get into the tiniest cracks and crevices. A sandstorm blinds, and a sand dune is a place of danger. The hot colors of this card represent the desert landscape, which is barren and inhospitable. The desert can be a place where the extreme conditions can quickly overwhelm both man and beast, causing death.

Seed Thoughts

Free yourself

End enslavement

See through materialism

Key Symbols

Chains

Darkness

Demons

15 THE DEVIL

15 The Devil
Sand Dune Monster

FAR LEFT: *In the Golden Dawn card, the Devil towers over the weak people who are too concerned with acquiring possessions.*

LEFT: *The Sand Dune monster of the Santa Fe Devil card is able to infiltrate anywhere and cause great damage.*

XVI | The Tower

THE NATURE OF THE TOWER

The structure of buildings can easily represent the self. Attics and secret rooms represent unexplored chambers of the mind. Basements represent hidden secrets and forgotten memories. Stairs represent the way to a higher consciousness. Ancient buildings speak for an antiquity that the soul recognizes. Spiritual buildings speak for the innermost aspirations of the soul. A neglected building reveals a poverty of being. A grandiose building speaks of an overvalued sense of self-worth. These are the images of the dream life. This trump shows us a building in the act of being destroyed by fire.

The Tower of the Tarot is, however, unusual – its top is formed by a crown. The crown of the tower has been dramatically lifted by a bolt of lightening of explosive force. The symbolism of the crown draws our attention to the head and the mind. Lightning represents a natural power that is beyond our control. This trump shows us a moment when the individual has been struck by a truth with the force of a thunderbolt. The revelation is so powerful that it breaks open the mind and shatters the lifestyle that has been.

Dramatic Change

This trump portrays the situations in life when everything we have built up and hold dear is struck by a thunderbolt. It may be damaging revelations, an accident, or a terrible event that cause the anguish. Collapse and reconstruction are inevitable. In Tibetan Buddhism, the thunderbolt symbolizes enlightenment – a dramatic moment of truth that shatters our normal understanding. However, this trump also signifies those unwelcome thunderbolts that strike our lives to the foundations. When this happens we have no choice but to rebuild and start again.

ABOVE: *The owl is an ancient bad omen, appearing on this trump to reinforce the card's symbolism of shocking events.*

The Tower as a Soul Friend

The Tower will support you when an aspect of your life collapses into ruins. The Tower tumbles to the ground, but its base stands firm and can be used to support a new structure. It will remind you not to lose heart, and that you can build a life that better reflects the new image that you have of yourself. Accept help from others to help you overcome your difficulties.

Marseilles Tarot Tower

Russian Tarot Tower

LEFT: *The top of the Tower is often shown to be shaped like a crown, linking it to the head and mind.*

Divinatory Significance

This trump indicates an unexpected change of circumstance – perhaps the collapse of hopes and expectations, a business failure, a divorce, or a breakdown of some kind. There is a need to rebuild and rethink direction and purpose.

Reversed

When reversed, this card indicates that the effects of collapse are slightly lessened. Perhaps you were well-prepared or had alternative plans in hand already. It also shows insecurity.

THE TOWER FROM THE MARSEILLES TAROT

The Tower in this Tarot is called the God-House. It is sometimes said that the body is the temple for the spirit. The God-House represents the life where divinity dwells. The three windows could perhaps stand for mind, body, and spirit. These, too, will fall and need to be repaired. Any crisis of faith demands some soul-searching, where everything is questioned and examined. When deconstruction of this nature is finished, then the reconstruction can begin.

THE TOWER FROM THE RUSSIAN TAROT

This trump has taken on an especially Russian nature. We see a Russian bell-tower that has exploded from within. Its contents, symbolizing the very essence of Russian life through the state, Church, and society, have been flung far and wide. The imperial crown, the cross and chalice, a censor, golden coins, and the *kvosh*, the typical Russian drinking vessel, have all been thrown from the tower. The symbolism of revolution is clear. This tower represents the people of Russia herself.

Seed Thoughts

Rebuild life

Reconstruct yourself

Arise like a phoenix

Key Symbols

The crown

The lightning bolt

The foundation

XVII | The Star

ABOVE: *The sign of Aquarius, the water-bearer, is also shared by the star goddess Nuit.*

BELOW: *This 1660 Folio Atlas of the Heavens shows an early fascination with astronomy.*

THE NATURE OF THE STAR

Every civilization, great and small, has looked up to the skies with curiosity and passion. Astronomy and astrology are the twin lenses through which we gaze at the stars. Astronomy takes us into observed learning; astrology takes us into myth and sacred psychology. The nature of any star is a fascinating enigma. However we choose to look at the heavens – with the eyes of a child, the vision of a poet, the telescope of an astronomer, the quest of a cosmologist – we are pondering the nature of the stars. Our questions and musing have produced many answers. The astrophysicists can describe the life of a star and analyze its make-up. The poet may see a divine metaphor.

The Mysteries of Time and Space

As we look up to the heavens, we are looking at a distant history, an image reflecting the passing of light years. We are looking back into time. No wonder, then, that the stars have always inspired and will continue to do so.

The Star as Soul Friend

The Star will support you when you reach out to the infinite and seek a connection to the vastness of a greater creation. The Star bestows a spiritual blessing that expands and universalizes your consciousness. Aquarius the water-bearer and Nuit the star goddess share the sign of two wavy lines. Read the star stories of the past and meditate under the night sky.

Divinatory Significance

This trump signifies your dreams, visions, and hopes at their most spiritual. These are the dreams that you most want to happen, yet they seem so remote as to be unattainable. Hold on to your dream. Keep the inspiration that gives you the drive to continue. Believe in your cherished wishes.

Reversed

When reversed, this card indicates that your talent is defeated by lack of vision. Perhaps poor self-image or low self-esteem stops you from holding the vision. Instead, you feel a sense of limitation and enclosure.

LEFT: *An Egyptian tomb painting showing the goddess Nuit swallowing the sun at night to give birth to it again in the morning.*

THE STAR FROM THE EGYPTIAN TAROT

Many Egyptian monuments and temples contain astronomical images and star alignments. The Great Pyramid is aligned to the heavens. In the Egyptian Tarot, the heavens are depicted as the naked star goddess, Nuit. She takes waters from the Nile to pour onto the land in a gesture that brings life to the lotus blooms and inspires the butterfly to take wing. The Nile was the life-blood at the heart of Egypt, thought to reflect an image of that other starry river, the Milky Way. The seven-pointed star with its seven companions stands for the multitude of stars in the kingdom of Nuit.

THE STAR FROM THE THOTH TAROT

In the distant background a seven-pointed star of Venus spins out into space. In the foreground a cosmic figure with raised arms pours starlight from an upturned chalice. She is Nuit, lady of stars. Behind her a planet floats in space, interlaced with a grid of starlight. In one corner we see roses and butterflies; crystalline structures fill the foreground. This shows our intimate connection with space. The exploding heavens and the constant activity of deep space spews out the raw materials of life as elements and molecules.

Seed Thoughts

Reach out to the infinite

Contemplate space

Extend your vision

Key Symbols

Nuit

The stars

Aquarius

Egyptian Tarot Star

The Star from the Thoth Tarot

XVIII | The Moon

THE NATURE OF THE MOON

Have you ever observed the moon? It is clear from archaeological evidence that thousands of years ago our ancestors watched the moon regularly and made a tally. This lunar count probably provided the first notation system. The moon was the first means of measuring the passage of time. The first calendars were based on the moon's cycles. The divinities related to the moon often have connections with time.

The moon has no light of its own. The dark of the new moon, the two crescent moons, and the full moon all reflect the amount of sunlight falling on it at any time. The moon completes its cycle every 29½ days. This cycle is shown in the lunar crown, which is composed of the two crescents and the full moon. This is worn by lunar goddesses and their priestesses to emphasize the centrality of this cycle for women.

The Silver Light

We should not underestimate the physical effects of the moon – its presence is enough to draw back the waters in tidal flow and have a measurable impact on growing plants. Some plants become especially attuned to its rhythmic patterns.

The phases of the moon may even affect our ability to heal after surgery. The body of moon lore has much to teach. This wisdom has always been in the hands of women, who are naturally attuned to cycle, transformation, and change. The moon has always been associated with hidden realms of dreams, magic-making, precognition, clairvoyance, and other psychic abilities. Such gifts develop only slowly. The small voice of intuitive knowing is fragile and needs to be nurtured into fullness.

The Moon as Soul Friend

The moon makes an easy soul companion. When you seek the lunar kingdom of the psychic and the spiritual, take the image of the moon goddess Luna as a guide. Come to know the moon's phases and movements from meditative observation. This will link you to all those who watched the moon and marked its phases so long ago.

BELOW: *The lunar cycle takes a month. The words "month" and "moon" are probably derived from the same root.*

The Moon from the Zolar Tarot

Santa Fe Tarot Moon

Divinatory Significance

This trump reminds you of the lunar forces in your life. Something hidden in your psyche may be trying to surface, perhaps through your dreams. Be aware that moonlight provides many opportunities for deception and mistakes. It is not a good time for making precise judgments, since hidden elements may still be concealed.

Reversed

When reversed, this card brings a clearer connection with the lunar powers. A good time for developing psychic interests and finding yourself in touch with inspiration. It can also mean obsession, phobias, fear and addiction are possible.

THE MOON FROM THE ZOLAR TAROT

In this card we see the evolutionary path. In the foreground is a pool from which a primitive creature emerges. In the background is a path that eventually passes between two towers. The dogs represent the development of mammals. The towers have been created by a developed consciousness. The moon watches all and time passes. This card reminds us that the moon is connected with nature.

THE MOON FROM THE SANTA FE TAROT

In Navaho tradition the moon is drawn in a sand painting to evoke the sacred powers. The moon is depicted as a pale replica of the sun. In Navaho mythology both the sun and moon are given feathers, which are dropped at regular intervals. Here we see the moon wearing dyed eagle feathers as a headdress and a collar, which the moon will drop on its course. This trump emphasizes the relationship between the sun and the moon.

ABOVE: *Luna, the moon goddess, is inspirational when trying to develop your spiritual side.*

Seed Thoughts

Follow the moon

Enjoy the dream

Relate to ebb and flow

Awaken the inner mind

Honor the phases

Key Symbols

Moonlight

Water

The ancestors

The divinities of the moon

XIX | The Sun

THE NATURE OF THE SUN

One of the first things that children draw is a layer of blue sky and a smiling sun. It is a cliché to repeat the many qualities of being that the sun has come to symbolize for so many different cultures. With the tearing of the ozone layer, perhaps for the first time in history sunshine has begun to pose a threat. Previously the sun and its light have always been seen as agents of life growth, well-being, and happiness. It has long been associated with kingship, being the focal point of the kingdom. Art of the Armana period under the Pharaoh Akhenaten drew the sun with extending rays ending in hands. Egyptian kings were identified with Horus, the golden hawk of the sun. Louis XIV saw himself as the Sun King with a court revolving around his central presence.

Here Comes the Sun

The sun is the light of the world that sustains all life. Unlike the moon, which shows us its changing faces, the sun is a constant light. Yet our relationship with it moves through a constant cycle that establishes seasonal change and the daily rhythm of darkness and light. The eastern sunrise has become a universal symbol of beginnings and arising. The sunset in the west symbolizes closure and departure. The eastern bank of the Nile is dedicated to life; the western bank of the Nile is the resting place for the dead. The apparent path of the sun has laid out the structure of the year into patterns of light and dark. The summer and winter solstice are the longest and the shortest days of the year. The equinoxes at spring and fall mark the days and nights of equal length.

The Sun as Soul Friend

The Sun will support you when you are ready to relax and enjoy yourself with friends and family. This is a trump of celebration and holiday spirit. If you have been working too hard, meditate on the Sun and the idea of rebirth.

ABOVE: *A beautifully illustrated alchemic treatise from the 16th century on the splendor of the sun.*

BELOW RIGHT: *King Louis XIV of France (1638–1715) was known as the Sun King. He ruled for 72 years.*

The Motherpeace Tarot Sun

The Sun from the Golden Dawn Tarot

Divinatory Significance

This trump indicates a time of happiness, accomplishment and fulfillment. You are doing well in whatever area you have chosen to pursue. Good luck seems to surround you. You feel carefree. You are enjoying life and all the things that it has to offer.

Reversed

When reversed, this trump indicates the loss of happiness and a reversal of your fortunes. The sun does not shine for you. You feel depressed at the outlook. You long for a change.

THE SUN FROM THE MOTHERPEACE TAROT

The Motherpeace Tarot shows us a scene of happiness and celebration. People of all races join hands and share the universal pleasure of sunshine. Balloons add to the party atmosphere. The whole card is bathed in the yellow of the sun, a color we naturally find mentally stimulating. Solar consciousness is the consciousness of the day, not the night, so it signifies a shared mind that permits communication and exchange. The butterfly superimposed against the sun is placed to represent the rebirth of a new group consciousness.

THE SUN FROM THE GOLDEN DAWN TAROT

The Golden Dawn Tarot shows two naked children holding hands beneath the sun. They are encircled by a stone wall that represents the zodiac. The girl stands in water, the boy on land. The card shows us the four elements of life: earth, air, fire, and water. These two figures represent humanity joined beneath the sun. Daisylike flowers with sun faces bloom.

Seed Thoughts

Be happy

Rejoice

Celebrate

Shine like the sun

Key Symbols

The central light

The heart of life

XX | Judgment

ABOVE: *The Egyptian Tarot card features people awakening at the sound of a heavenly trumpet.*

ABOVE: *The Hebrew letter* Shin *signifies spiritual fire. It appears in the foreground of the Golden Dawn card.*

THE NATURE OF JUDGMENT

The threat of the Last Judgment was once held over the lives of god-fearing folk like an eternal sword of Damocles. This concept still holds true in some circles, but this trump is not a depiction of the last judgment – just the opposite, in fact. What we see depicted here is the first awakening to the spiritual life. It is the first response to the voice of the spirit. We see an angelic figure that represents higher consciousness. The angel sounds the trumpet – not to awaken the dead, but to awaken the living!

Awakening

Awakening can take many forms: some have an inborn sense of knowing; others come to spiritual awakening later, often through a crisis precipitated by a grand failure in material life; others just come gradually, as life shows itself to be a spiritual enterprise. There are many paths to the place of awakening: significant events, meetings with key people, conversations, books, encounters, dreams. Everyone has their own story to tell.

Judgment as Soul Friend

Judgment will support you when you hear the clarion call to awake in whatever form it comes to you. It will bring the desire to live with greater consciousness and awareness. The transformation from sleep to wakefulness is gradually accomplished. It is seeded in the mindfulness of daily activities and comes to fruition in the birth of a new and expansive consciousness.

Divinatory Significance

This trump represents an increased awareness and use of personal powers. It indicates a release from limiting thoughts and old belief systems. There is a strong desire to be transformed and to develop.

Reversed

When reversed, this card indicates an unwillingness to hear the voice of spiritual liberation. You prefer the safety of the known and the familiar. Waking implies personal responsibility and the falling away of cherished illusions.

JUDGMENT FROM THE THOTH TAROT

The Thoth Tarot shows us the same theme magnified to a grand scale. It represents the awakening of the group.

Crowley called this trump the Aeon. It is a card of great prophetic insight. We see the body of the star goddess Nuit enveloping the child of the future age, who sets foot on the letter Shin with its triple yods. Within each of the flames is a human form waiting to rise with the birth of the new age. Crowley wrote, "The time for the birth of an aeon seems to be indicated by the great concentration of political power with the accompanying improvements in the means of travel and communication, with a general advance in philosophy and science, with a general need of consolidated religious thought." Is this a picture of the time in which we now find ourselves? Is this the time of mass awakening as a prelude to the birth of the aeon?

JUDGMENT FROM THE GOLDEN DAWN TAROT

The Judgment card from the Golden Dawn Tarot shows us the moment of awakening. We see an angelic figure sounding a trumpet from within the loop of a spiral and serpent set in the sky. Perhaps your name is carried through this vibration. In the world below, several naked figures stand immersed in the waters of life. In a baptismal moment, the sound is heard and the seeds of spiritual awakening take on a new potency. One figure arises triumphantly from a coffin. In the foreground of the Golden Dawn trump, we see the Hebrew letter *Shin*, which signifies elemental fire as spirit. This letter is written as three interconnected flames, each one the separate letter *yod*, individually signifying spiritual fire. This trump is painting us a picture of spiritual birth.

Seed Thoughts

Personal awakening

Mass initiation

The birth of the New Age

Key Symbols

Higher consciousness

Mindfulness

Thoth Tarot Judgment

Golden Dawn Tarot Judgment

XXI | The World

ABOVE: *The Hubble telescope has allowed us to increase our knowledge of the wonders of the universe.*

THE NATURE OF THE WORLD

We now come to the final trump, the World. We have been the first generation to view the world from space. The famous image of the world has become an icon of our time. No previous generation has looked upon the world in this way. This final trump asks us to extend our vision of reality as our horizons shift continuously. Where this trump was once named the World, more recent decks have renamed it the Universe. Renaissance commentators could not have shared this sense of expansion and connection. The move into space as the new frontier will no doubt continue into the next millennium and stretch our understanding of our place in creation even more.

Global Consciousness

Exploration into outer space has contributed immeasurably to an extended view of the infinite expanses beyond planet Earth. The Hubble telescope has revealed wonders on a scale previously difficult to envisage. Planet Earth is a part of a great unfolding cosmic drama. We are touched by cosmic winds and affected by sunspots and solar flares. Earth is part of a wider cosmic family. As the 21ST century dawns, we are ready to see ourselves nestled in a creation of extraordinary wonder and infinite possibility.

The World as Soul Friend

The World will support you when you seek to expand your horizons, whether physical or mental. Travel may be indicated in connection with a creative project or with business. This trump will support you in developing a sense of community and extended family. This trump is a doorway into a universalized and continuously expanding consciousness. It brings global awareness and a global conscience.

Divinatory Significance

This trump indicates involvement: positive partnerships with others, possibly travel, or pursuits and activities that expand and enlarge your understanding of the world – a time of success when you cannot put a foot wrong. You feel that some unseen force is supporting and guiding you.

LEFT: *The* moebus: *inner and outer surface are part of the same continuum. It appears on the Thoth World card.*

Motherpeace Tarot World

Reversed

When reversed, this trump indicates a partial success. Perhaps your plans were not quite bold enough to sustain a broad vision. It also shows low self-esteem.

THE WORLD FROM THE MOTHERPEACE TAROT

The Motherpeace Tarot again shows us a dancing figure. She dances with tambourine in one hand and raised torch in the other. The uplifted torch is reminiscent of the symbolism at the opening ceremony of the Olympic games, where the family of humanity meet in peace and cooperation. Here the boundaries of the circle are formed by naked figures of every color holding one another in a simple gesture of support and interdependence. A garland of flowers is strung across the circle. This is a picture of joyful celebration and cooperative humanity.

The Thoth World card

THE WORLD FROM THE THOTH TAROT

The World card from the Thoth Tarot gives us a beautiful image of continuing and unfolding creation. Elegant spiral forms interpenetrate space. The Four Holy Kerubs, the living expression of the four elements of Earth, Air, Fire, and Water, stand sentinel in each of the corners. The World dancer has become entwined in the ecstatic dance of creation as she stretches within the opening coils of a spiraling serpent. Behind her we see the mathematical enigma of the *moebus*, a figure where inner and outer surface are part of the same continuum. Beneath her stands the skeletal plan of the house of Matter, describing the 92 known elements. Stars are spread upon an elliptical path. The World trump is a symbolic expression of the forces of creation: this card might be thought of as a representation of the bubble chamber where subatomic particles collide and pass in a magical dance of continuous creation.

Seed Thoughts

Creation unfolds

Consciousness expands

As above so below

Think globally, act locally

Key Symbols

Holistic philosophy

One world

Interconnection

The Four Elements

THE FOUR AND THE ONE

The four elements are found in many quite different spiritual traditions, from ancient alchemy to contemporary shamanism. If you look at the world, this is not really surprising. Earth, air, fire, and water are life-sustaining powers when they are in balance, although an excess of any one of them can become potentially life-destroying. They may appear quite separate, but the elements often mingle. Water is invisibly carried in the air. Fire (as the power of the sun) touches the earth and is absorbed by plants. Fire feeds on oxygen. Water contains oxygen. These interconnections take us closer to understanding the true interdependence of all forms of life.

ABOVE: *The four elements are also reminiscent of the four seasons. A fifth element – Akasa – binds them all together.*

RIGHT: *Contemporary shamanism takes account of the four elements in its beliefs and practices.*

THE INVISIBLE
FIFTH ELEMENT

In keeping with the idea of unity, the four elements are rarely depicted in isolation, and usually as quarters of a circle that encompasses them all and suggests the four-season cycle of the year. At the center, where the four elements meet, a point is naturally created. This fifth point can represent the fifth element, *Akasa*, which is invisible yet ever-present. At the same time, the fifth element could be seen in the wholeness of the circle. As soon as we think symbolically, we can hold two paradoxical ideas at the same time.

*Cups are associated with water,
Cancer, Scorpio, and Pisces.*

THINKING METAPHORICALLY

Thinking literally and thinking symbolically are two quite different things. If we look only literally at the four elements, we move toward a scientific analysis. If we think symbolically, we move toward a poetic and metaphorical understanding. This is the mode of all spiritual traditions, so think symbolically about the following questions:

- What qualities of being or character do you associate with earth?
- What qualities of being or character do you associate with air?
- What qualities of being or character do you associate with fire?
- What qualities of being or character do you associate with water?
- To which element would you relate the following:
  a sunny disposition, a melancholy outlook, a winter's day, a flowing brook, a thunderstorm, a planning session, a love affair, a raging fight, a spring afternoon, midnight?

*Swords are associated with air,
Gemini, Libra, and Aquarius.*

ASTROLOGY, ELEMENTS, AND THE SUITS OF THE TAROT

In astrology, the twelve signs of the zodiac are divided into the four elements. The elemental signs make another natural traveling companion to the Tarot. The Hermetic Tarot decks invariably incorporate astrological symbolism into the design of the cards. The astrological signature is used to reinforce and extend the associations related to each of the cards.

*Disks are associated with earth,
Taurus, Virgo, and Capricorn.*

Traditional Tarot represents Earth by a pentacle, Air by a sword, Fire by a rod, and Water by a cup. This is one approach, but there are of course many others. The familiar symbols of the four suits have carried particular connotations for other generations. Pietro Aretino in *The Talking Cards*, written in the mid-16TH century, related the suits to gambling. Swords recalled those who died through gaming. Staves depicted the punishment for cheats. Cups represented wine as the inevitable table companion. Coins represented the bag of coins put up as the stake. In our own time, we have become more accustomed to the four symbols being used to represent the four quarters of the year, the four elements, and the four Jungian functions.

*Wands are associated with fire,
Aries, Leo, and Sagittarius.*

Earth

THE ELEMENT OF EARTH

The element of earth is represented by the astrological signs of Taurus, Virgo, and Capricorn. We walk on the earth. Our houses are rooted on the earth. We live on the earth, but do we ever stop to think about our relationship with this foundation? Think for a moment of the many resources that the people of the world use. These come from the earth, whether as mineral deposit or as natural power source. The earth provides every resource that we have recreated, recombined, reshaped through agriculture, industry, and production. Humanity has had a powerful effect on the earth. Currently the nature of our shared relationship is a cause for concern. This element draws our attention to the cycles of nature, increase, and abundance. It asks us to look at our relationship and attitude to the resources that we own, both individually and collectively. Nature offers many lessons in balance and economy.

THE SUIT OF DISKS, COINS, STONES

The meaning of the disk or coin is unequivocal. We all understand the medium of exchange. In a society geared to exchange, we all know the value of money. The coin as symbol of this suit represents the sphere of activity covered by commerce, business, and trade. It represents our dealings with the world, our attitude to resources, and how we choose to use what comes our way. The pentacle inscribed upon the disk reminds us that spirit and matter cannot be separated. It expresses a unity that is often lost in the world of work, where the determining factor is simply the profit margin.

The stone is a wonderful symbol for the enduring qualities of this element. The next time you pick up a stone, wonder about its age against yours. Where has this stone been? Where will it be in a hundred years' time, or perhaps even a thousand years' time? The Santa Fe Tarot uses the buffalo as its image for elemental earth. What more profound symbol could be chosen to show waste and desecration of Nature's gift? The buffalo once supported a way of life by providing every resource, both spiritual and material. Herds of buffalo once took days to pass. Now their time has passed. Here is a perfect symbol for the element of earth, which deserves our meditation.

ABOVE: *We do not always value the earth as we should, inflicting damage and stripping resources.*

RIGHT: *The earth element is associated with the astrological signs Taurus, Virgo, and Capricorn.*

Taurus

Virgo

Capricorn

The Suit of Disks by Name and Astrological Signature

The Ace of Disks	– The Root of the Powers of Earth	
The Two of Disks	– Change	– Jupiter in Capricorn
The Three of Disks	– Work	– Mars in Capricorn
The Four of Disks	– Power	– Sun in Capricorn
The Five of Disks	– Worry	– Venus in Taurus
The Six of Disks	– Success	– Moon in Taurus
The Seven of Disks	– Failure	– Saturn in Taurus
The Eight of Disks	– Prudence	– Sun in Virgo
The Nine of Disks	– Gain	– Venus in Virgo
The Ten of Disks	– Wealth	– Mercury in Virgo

We will meet these ten faces of elemental earth again when we look at the significance of the numbered cards in more detail.

Air

THE ELEMENT OF AIR

The element of air is represented by the astrological signs of Aquarius, Gemini, and Libra. Air is invisible, yet omnipresent and shared. It is a wonderful symbol of unity. We interact with the air with every breath, yet we never stop to think about it. We share the air we breathe with each other. The mind is invisible, yet like air it is clearly present through its action. The winds that circulate around the world have been a great force in navigation. Wind is a motive power that we can harness. Mind is also a motive power that we can harness and channel. The sail and the windmill show us wind power at work. We see a direct relationship between the strength of the wind and the resulting degree of power. We have learned to harness nature's power with considerable success, yet we have not learned to master the domain of the mind – it still remains an incompletely understood territory. Perhaps when the unity of mind, body, and spirit is fully understood, a new day will dawn for us all.

THE SUIT OF SWORDS, ARROWS, LIGHTNING

The sword is the Hermetic symbol for the element of air and the powers of the mind. Few wield a sword these days. It has been relegated almost entirely to ceremonial or theatrical use. Ceremony reveals the power of the sword as symbol of state. Theater shows us the power of the sword to kill and maim, defend and protect. Its use depends entirely upon our intent. Like a sword, we may use the mind to defend or destroy, analyze, or attack. The sharp tongue is like the sharpened jabbing at the weaknesses of the enemy. A razor-sharp mind is a powerful weapon; it cleaves truth from falsehood and cuts through deception instantly.

ABOVE: *Air is vital and invisible, yet demonstrates force through the power of the wind. It can be likened to the powers of the mind.*

RIGHT: *Air is linked with the suit of Swords. Swords are associated with communication and arguments.*

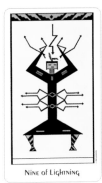

NINE OF LIGHTNING

LEFT: *The Santa Fe Tarot uses lightning for the suit of Swords.*

RIGHT: *The astrological signs linked to the suit of Swords and the air element.*

Aquarius

Gemini

Libra

The Medicine Woman Tarot chooses to use the symbolism of the arrow for this suit. Not only is this in keeping with Native American traditions, but this symbolism provides a new set of associations. Like the sword, the arrow moves through the air and can be used to defend or attack. For the arrow to be effective, it requires a target. Every word that falls short of the target is a wasted word. Perhaps where the sword serves to symbolize the broader sweep of the mind, the arrow better represents the value of each word. The effective archer trains mind and body, hand and eye to develop coordination. If we apply the same discipline and training to the mind, we can become effective and potent communicators – the arrow will hit its mark. The Santa Fe Tarot uses the symbolism of lightning to describe this suit. This symbol is in keeping with a tradition born in the open expanses, where lightning is still an awesome natural phenomenon. Lightning combines both light and power with instant directional force. Can your thoughts be compared to lightning?

The Suit of Swords by Name and Astrological Signature

The Ace of Swords	–	The Root of the Powers of Air		
The Two of Swords	–	Peace	–	Moon in Libra
The Three of Swords	–	Sorrow	–	Saturn in Libra
The Four of Swords	–	Truce	–	Jupiter in Libra
The Five of Swords	–	Defeat	–	Venus in Aquarius
The Six of Swords	–	Science	–	Mercury in Aquarius
The Seven of Swords	–	Futility	–	Moon in Gemini
The Eight of Swords	–	Interference	–	Jupiter in Gemini
The Nine of Swords	–	Cruelty	–	Mars in Gemini
The Ten of Swords	–	Ruin	–	Sun in Gemini

We will meet these ten faces of elemental air again when we look at the significance of the numbered cards in more detail.

Checkpoint

The following qualities and activities are associated with the element of air:

- *craftsmanship*
- *construction*
- *ideas*
- *worries*
- *serious decisions*
- *delays*
- *disappointments*
- *losses*
- *separations*
- *matters that require a specialist*
- *impulsiveness*
- *property and possessions*
- *recklessness*
- *using natural resources*
- *status*
- *practical application*
- *manufacture*

Fire

ABOVE: *Fire is a source of heat and light, but is a destructive force that must be controlled.*

BELOW: *A staff was used for support; in Tarot it symbolizes a link between the temporal and the spiritual.*

THE ELEMENT OF FIRE

The element of fire is represented by the astrological signs of Leo, Sagittarius, and Aries. Imagine the moment when two flints spark and fire is struck – our ancestors could conjure up this magic with great skill. Nowadays, we take fire for granted. The coming of fire so revolutionized human life that its appearance was encapsulated in the story of Prometheus, who stole it from the gods to give to humanity. Fire gives both heat and light. We have learned to control and channel heat to drive and fuel technology. We have delighted in candlelight and sacred flame. Fire purifies and consumes, transforms and releases. The mythical firebird, the phoenix, even reminds us that fire can be purging and renewing.

All life on earth is sustained by the sun. Earthly fire reflects this cosmic fire. Fire is an active element – it leaps over gaps and firebreaks like a living creature. Fire is never still, never restful, always dynamic. We see ourselves mirrored in the nature of fire. We, too, can be restless and dangerous beings consumed by passions and powerful drives. We feel the fire of our own nature as physical passion, creative heat, and smoldering energy.

THE SUIT OF WANDS, RODS, PIPES, RAINBOWS

The element of fire is represented by the rod, wand, or baton in the Hermetic tradition. Unlike the cup, which is a familiar household object, the rod, baton, or staff has become unfamiliar. The nearest reference point may be the walking cane, which rather like a small staff can be used as a support or for clearing the path ahead. A lone hiker often takes along a good walking cane; the solitary hermit leans upon his staff. In the wrong hands the staff can be a weapon as well as a support. The archetypal magician with his wand wields a special force like a musical conductor who directs power with a rod or baton. The rod is inherently straight. It serves like a spine to support, direct, and connect two separate realms. The spine is also a conductor of life force, which is both sexual and sacred in nature. The serpent fire speaks through this element as burning inspiration, boundless creativity, driving energy, restless enthusiasm, radiant inner fire, and latent potential. The

ABOVE: *In Greek legend, Prometheus stole fire from the gods for man to use. Zeus punished him by having him chained to a rock and tortured by a vulture.*

Leo *Sagittarius* *Aries*

Navaho tradition expresses the qualities of fire through the symbolism of the rainbow, a magical light in the sky. Rainbow people are considered to be hasty, gift-giving people capable of great harmony and peace. The Medicine Woman Tarot takes the pipe as its symbol for this suit. The pipe conducts an energy from one place to another. The pipe can be likened to the spine and to the rod. As a hollow rod, it awaits what we choose to fill it with. The pipe of peace, always a sacrament, physically expresses the presence of fire in a harmonizing way.

The Suit of Wands by Name and Astrological Signature

The Ace of Wands	– The Root of the Powers of Fire	
The Two of Wands	– Dominion	– Mars in Aries
The Three of Wands	– Virtue	– Moon in Aries
The Four of Wands	– Completion	– Venus in Aries
The Five of Wands	– Strife	– Saturn in Leo
The Six of Wands	– Victory	– Jupiter in Leo
The Seven of Wands	– Valor	– Mars in Leo
The Eight of Wands	– Swiftness	– Mercury in Sagittarius
The Nine of Wands	– Strength	– Moon in Sagittarius
The Ten of Wands	– Oppression	– Saturn in Sagittarius

We will meet these ten faces of elemental fire again when we look at the significance of the numbered cards in more detail.

Checkpoint

The following qualities and activities are associated with the element of fire:

- *compassion*
- *movement*
- *fulfillment*
- *celebration*
- *desolation*
- *romance*
- *surprise*
- *energy*
- *enthusiasm*
- *communications*
- *letters*
- *phone calls*
- *distant travel*
- *enterprise*
- *the bank balance*
- *courage*

Water

Scorpio

THE ELEMENT OF WATER

The element of water is represented by the astrological signs of Scorpio, Pisces, and Cancer. Perhaps because our bodies are composed largely of water, we seem to have an innate love of water in its many forms. Oceans and streams, pools and ponds, lakes and rivers, each speak to us of possibility. In powerful mythological images such as the well of vision or the fountain of youth, the waters hold mysterious or hidden depths where both demons and delights may dwell. Its mirrorlike surface is the place where we see ourselves. To drink from the living waters is to partake of the waters of life as knowledge, wisdom, or inspiration.

The importance of water in human life has given it powerful symbolic overtones. Ritual cleansing and purification with water to wash away the old and welcome the new is universal and ancient. Renewal through water is a powerful rite of passage whether as baptism, bathing in a sacred river, or finally as sea burial. The reality and symbolism of water is deeply imbedded in us: we are moved to tears, and we each begin life suspended in a living sac of water. The element of water is experienced deeply by the soul.

ABOVE: *Ripples on the smooth surface of a crystal pool reflect the problems that can disturb the tranquility of life.*

ABOVE: *Water is linked with Cups, Cancer, Scorpio, and Pisces.*

THE SUIT OF CUPS

The element of water is invariably symbolized by the cup or the bowl. The cup is an everyday object, yet it also carries a profound significance. When the ordinary cup becomes the chalice; the context shifts from the mundane to the sacred. The cup is a container, it has no function without its contents. The loving cup is a shared cup. The Eucharist cup is a sacramental cup. The libation cup is an offering cup. The empty cup calls to be filled.

The drinking vessel must surely have been one of the earliest of all artifacts. Perhaps the cup developed from a simple hollowed gourd. Whatever its parentage, when we consider the cup we are reminded of the whole range of social and emotional interaction. Whether as a container for water or wine, the cup shows us the human being as a social animal. It is no surprise, then,

Pisces

Cancer

Checkpoint

The following qualities and activities are associated with the element of water:

- *feelings*
- *depth*
- *emotion*
- *business concerns*
- *negotiations*
- *sensitivity*
- *relationships*
- *caring*
- *love*
- *comfort*
- *friendship*
- *colleagues*
- *creative activities*

that the suit of cups represents human feelings in many forms, from the overflowing cup of happiness to the spilled cup of disappointment. The bowl shares much the same symbolism as the cup. It, too, is a container that holds and offers nourishment. It, too, is a grail that feeds the many.

The Suit of Cups by Name and Astrological Signature

The Ace of Cups	–	The Root of the Powers of Water	
The Two of Cups	–	Love	– Venus in Cancer
The Three of Cups	–	Abundance	– Mercury in Cancer
The Four of Cups	–	Luxury	– Moon in Cancer
The Five of Cups	–	Disappointment	– Mars in Scorpio
The Six of Cups	–	Pleasure	– Sun in Scorpio
The Seven of Cups	–	Debauch	– Venus in Scorpio
The Eight of Cups	–	Indolence	– Saturn in Pisces
The Nine of Cups	–	Happiness	– Jupiter in Pisces
The Ten of Cups	–	Satiety	– Mars in Pisces

We will meet these ten faces of elemental water again when we look at the significance of the numbered cards in more detail.

BELOW: *The River Ganges in India is sacred and people bathe in its water to purify themselves.*

The Aces

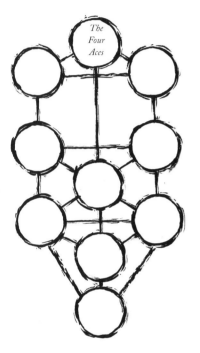

ABOVE: *The cards of the Minor Arcana are assigned a position on the Tree of Life. The Aces are on Kether, the Crown. These are very positive cards to receive in a spread.*

THE FOUR ACES ON THE TREE OF LIFE

The Aces are called the Roots of the Powers of their respective suits. Each one symbolizes a beginning that is charged with great potency and possibility. To encounter the Ace in a spread is a very positive omen. The Ace can indicate a change of circumstance that sets a new train of events in motion. All the Aces are like seeds, often insignificant in the moment, but rich with the promise of the future. We will look at the Aces in the Thoth Tarot.

THE ACE OF DISKS – THE ROOT OF THE POWERS OF EARTH

The Ace of Disks is a symbolic picture of the creation of matter. At the heart of the card are allusions to the key principles of sacred geometry. Aside from the intricacies of numerical symbolism, we see wings enfolded around an ovoid. This is the doorway of creation, described mathematically as a vesica.

Divinatory Significance

The Ace of Disks suggests tangible improvement, such as a new possibility, perhaps a new job prospect, a win, windfall, or unexpected bonus. It may suggest the beginning of a practical project.

Reversed

Money is delayed or a hoped-for project does not materialize.

THE ACE OF SWORDS – THE ROOT OF THE POWERS OF AIR

The Ace of Swords shows a sword waiting to be gained. Its hilt is facing toward us and its point reaches upward into the cosmos. It is crowned with 22 rays of light. The sword rises against a golden light and pushes away the clouds of confusion as it pierces the air.

Divinatory Significance

The emergence of a powerful idea or a plan, scheme, or possibility; a revelatory moment of great clarity and insight.

Thoth Ace of Disks *Thoth Ace of Swords* *Thoth Ace of Wands* *Thoth Ace of Cups*

Reversed

Keep a sense of proportion about your sense of vision. Don't antagonize others with your grandiose schemes.

THE ACE OF WANDS – THE ROOT OF THE POWERS OF FIRE

The Ace of Wands is the embodiment of fire. Each flame is portrayed in the form of the letter *Yod*, which signifies spiritual fire. Together they depict the Tree of Life. The colors of the card suggest a powerful energy. The image is of a ceremonial torch that is passed from person to person.

Divinatory Significance

The Ace of Wands suggests the beginning of a creative or artistic project based on new vision or inspiration.

Reversed

You will be keen to make a start, but delays and obstacles will appear.

THE ACE OF CUPS – THE ROOT OF THE POWERS OF WATER

The Ace of Cups shows a chalice that is rooted in an unfolding lotus, showing unfolding love. The chalice emanates radiance. Above the cup, descending into it, is the dove of light. This is the Christian symbol for the Holy Ghost and the pagan emblem of Aphrodite and Ishtar as goddesses of human love. The chalice represents the source of love in life.

Divinatory Significance

The Ace of Cups shows a positive beginning: a new friendship or supportive work association, love, and friendship, even the possibility of romance.

Reversed

You will be keen to make new friends or just get out more, but delays and obstacles will appear to thwart your hopes.

The Twos

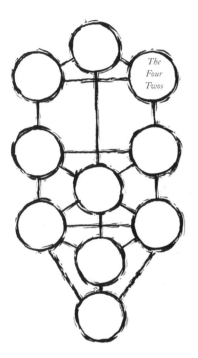

The
Four
Twos

THE FOUR TWOS ON THE TREE OF LIFE

From unity we move to a state of change. The single cell does not remain in a
unified state but divides itself into two. The Twos include the idea of balance,
harmony, and choice. Each of the Twos represents a quest for equilibrium in
its respective suit. We will look at the Twos in the Motherpeace Tarot.

THE TWO OF DISKS – CHANGE
– JUPITER IN CAPRICORN

A woman nurses two babies. She is held in a circle by a double-headed
snake. Jupiter represents the principle of expansion. Capricorn represents
practical application such as career, the workplace, and money management.
The double-headed snake signifies the double-edged nature of opportunity.
More work is only welcome when we have the time and capacity to fit it in,
otherwise, it becomes an unwelcome burden.

Divinatory Significance

The Two of Disks indicates that this is a time when a lot is happening. Extra
responsibilities seem to arrive on your doorstep. Here are the ups and downs
in life, such as having to juggle money carefully to get by.

Reversed

It may be difficult to cope with everything that is expected of you.

THE TWO OF SWORDS – PEACE – MOON IN LIBRA

A stork teaches a woman to balance while she dances with her sword. This
card is assigned to Libra, the card of balance, and shows the full moon,
which sheds a bright light on any situation. The woman has attained a point
of balance. She does not move.

Divinatory Significance

This is the weighing of one possibility against another. Indecision is here, for
the scales seem perfectly balanced. Perhaps an agreement to defer a solution
or decision until the future is possible.

Motherpeace Two of Disks

Motherpeace Two of Swords

Reversed

A decision has been taken, and change will follow.

THE TWO OF WANDS – DOMINION – MARS IN ARIES

A woman calls upon her ancestors for help. Here the other person belongs to the spirit or dream world, yet their presence is real enough. The card is attributed to Mars in Aries – a very fiery combination. We also see a woman in the act of striking fire.

Motherpeace Two of Wands

Divinatory Significance

Lots of energy. You know your own potential. A good time for action; a reliable partner may be just what you need to get something going.

Reversed

A sense of hope and anticipation, but the hoped-for goal is likely to fade on the horizon. Delays are indicated.

Motherpeace Two of Cups

THE TWO OF CUPS – LOVE – VENUS IN CANCER

In the Two of Cups two mermaids greet each other in the sea. They extend black and white chalices in a sign of mutual friendship. Two dolphins play beneath a crescent moon. The card draws upon many of the symbols connected with the element of water. We see the cup and the moon, water, and a predominance of the color blue. The mermaid is not an uncommon dream figure – it represents our unconscious submerged feelings.

Divinatory Significance

A partnership is being created in a reciprocal exchange of love. Here is harmony and peace, accord and joy. A harmonious balance.

Reversed

The failure of love. Infatuation has worn off – the parting of the ways or an ending of a friendship is signaled. Feelings of disconnection or loneliness.

The Threes

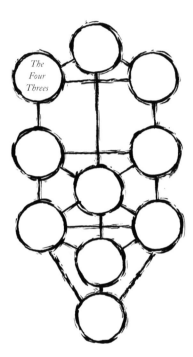

ABOVE: *The Threes are positioned on Binah, Understanding, a place redolent of feminine energy.*

THE FOUR THREES ON THE TREE OF LIFE

This represents the natural growth that follows the union of opposites, symbolized by the Great Mother who is called Binah. This is the place of archetypal feminine yin energy – which is said to be receptive in contrast to the yang energy, which is dynamic. We will look at the Threes in the Russian Tarot.

THE THREE OF DISKS – WORK – MARS IN CAPRICORN

Here is a master craftsman, a musician who is about to play the balalaika as his wealthy patron looks on. His skills as musician and craftsman should be appreciated. Mars represents physical energy, Capricorn represents practical activity. Together they provide the drive required to master a skill.

Divinatory Significance

Here we see the results of hard work and of the opportunity to show what one can do. The laborer is rewarded: hard work, talent, and application are paying off. Achievement in one's chosen career.

Reversed

Shoddy work and insufficient application bring meager recognition.

THE THREE OF SWORDS –
SORROW – SATURN IN LIBRA

Three swords hang over a heart. Bells hang in the background. Bells ring to mark both sorrow and joy. Can there be one without the other? Libra is the sign of balance, but Saturn brings a heaviness that outweighs all.

Divinatory Significance

Heartache, sorrow, and a time for endings. Bitter words have caused much pain. May also indicate physical heart problems.

Reversed

Separation and loss. The beginning of recovery. Is there something to be learned about yourself from this?

ABOVE: *Yin and Yang are opposite energies: Yin is passive, and Yang is active. The Threes are allied to Yin.*

Three of Coins

Russian Three of Disks

Three of Swords

Russian Three of Swords

THE THREE OF WANDS – VIRTUE – SUN IN ARIES

A man looks to the distant horizon. His clothing shows him to be a *boyar*, one of the wealthy land-owning merchants who exercised great power in Russia's history. In the background is a ship that symbolizes trade, activity, and possible good fortune. The sign of Aries represents a dynamic, potent, and determined energy.

Divinatory Significance

Good news is likely. Travel in connection with work is on the horizon. Teamwork and cooperation has paid off.

Reversed

A man looks toward the same horizon, but in vain. The ships will land elsewhere, and the expected opportunity will not transpire, leading to disappointment and energy expended in vain.

Three of Clubs

Russian Three of Wands

Three of Cups

Russian Three of Cups

THE THREE OF CUPS – ABUNDANCE – MERCURY IN CANCER

Three girls in colorful costumes dance in celebration. We see ornate bowls that are probably full of wine. Mercury represents the ability to communicate. Cancer is a water sign representing feelings. There is a sense of giving vent to the emotions through words and actions.

Divinatory Significance

Here is delight and joy. The girls dance with joyful exuberance. This signifies a celebration, a time for friends, family, and loved ones – a party perhaps, or possible connections to a wedding.

Reversed

You can have too much of a good thing. Take care, don't overdo the good times, you will regret the indulgence afterward.

The Fours

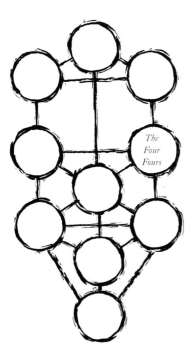

THE FOUR FOURS ON THE TREE OF LIFE

The Fours are associated with Mercy; a sense of retreat to a place of safety. Additionally, the number four is related to stability and security, which reinforces the stability inherent in the element of earth and the suit of Disks. This underlying stability is shared by all the Fours. We will look at the Fours in the Zolar Tarot.

THE FOUR OF DISKS – POWER – SUN IN CAPRICORN

A man is seated on a block. Both feet are planted on large disks. He cradles another disk between his upper and lower arms. He wears a fourth disk as a crown. There is a city behind him in the background. The Sun in Capricorn indicates qualities of hard work, application, worldly ambition, and financial flair. Such qualities make powerful assets in commerce.

Divinatory Significance

Here is a man rooted in his work and its reward. Here is economic and financial stability. But don't be too possessive about what you have.

Reversed

The control that you are looking for seems to evade you. Financial insecurity. Money slips through your fingers.

THE FOUR OF CUPS – LUXURY – MOON IN CANCER

A man is seated by a tree. He seems lost in thought. A cup appears magically and is extended to him. What does this mean? What is being offered here? Is this a poisoned chalice or the cup of happiness? He pauses to consider its implications. Just as the moon is hidden from us during daylight, our deepest wishes can be hidden or illusory, too. The sign of Cancer represents the feelings and our need for emotional security.

Divinatory Significance

Take the time to reflect on life. Something new is being offered. This is not the time to make a rushed decision. It is time to look at what is really important.

Gain in speculative matters. Possible legacy or a gift of money.

4 ♦ THE FOUR OF PENTACLES

MINOR ARCANA

Obstacles and delays with possible loss of material possessions.

Zolar Four of Disks

Recovery from an illness. Improvement in personal affairs.

4 ♠ THE FOUR OF SWORDS

MINOR ARCANA

Avoid arguments with associates. Economize on your daily expenditures.

Zolar Four of Swords

A new romance. A prosperous undertaking.

4 ♣ THE FOUR OF WANDS

MINOR ARCANA

News of a birth. Increase in income.

Zolar Four of Wands

A desire for a change that should be carefully considered. Indecision about a new venture.

4 ♥ THE FOUR OF CUPS

MINOR ARCANA

A change in your present plans. A new association that will prove troublesome.

Zolar Four of Cups

Reversed

The time for reflection has passed. Now is the time to re-emerge and take up the reins again, without indulging in self-pity.

THE FOUR OF SWORDS – TRUCE – JUPITER IN LIBRA

The knight is an image of activity and dynamism, but here we see his effigy, asking us to slow down and look at two opposing forces running through life. Jupiter brings expansion in activities, ideas, concerns, and involvement. Libra reminds us to balance these against health, rest, and general well-being.

Divinatory Significance

We see a knight in repose. It is a time for recuperation, or retreat. Perhaps a vacation is needed. A period of mental rest would be beneficial. Possibly a connection with hospitals, unless we make time for rest and recovery.

Reversed

Renewed action is possible. A return to the fray with restored energy.

THE FOUR OF WANDS – COMPLETION – VENUS IN ARIES

Here we see a castle, but after all, "Every man's home is his castle." The family home is decked for a celebration. Garlands have been made. Girls dance. Venus relates to our happiness and joy. Aries represents the fiery drive to "be." Together, Venus in Aries represent a zest for life and a *joie de vivre* that lets us know it's good to be alive.

Divinatory Significance

Success and delight, celebration and satisfaction. There is something to celebrate: perhaps a new house, putting down roots, or an anniversary.

Reversed

Nothing can spoil the day. The spirit of celebration is genuine.

ABOVE: *The Zolar Tarot spells out the associated playing card suits: Disks/Diamonds, Swords/Spades, Wands/Clubs, Cups/Hearts.*

The Fives

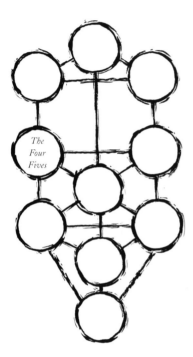

ABOVE: *The Fives are placed on Geburah (Severity), a destructive branch on the Tree of Life.*

The Four Fives

THE FOUR FIVES ON THE TREE OF LIFE

The negative connotations of all the Fives are associated with breakdown and disintegration, the decay that follows ripeness. Breakdown eventually comes to every civilization. We will look at the Fives in the Scapini Tarot.

THE FIVE OF SWORDS –
DEFEAT – VENUS IN AQUARIUS

A man sprawls on the floor in an opium-induced stupor. Chaos erupts all around, but he does not notice. The hilts of five swords have taken the shapes of demons and vampires. Venus represents our desire for joy. Aquarius represents the collective mind. Seeking higher consciousness through inappropriate means brings only delusion.

Divinatory Significance

Here is a time of tension and unpleasantness. There is a desire to escape. Cruel words are in the air. Revenge and gamesmanship are the order of the day. Watch out for underhanded dealing.

Reversed

Little improvement. Uncertain outlook, weakness, misfortune. But who is the victim? Something will be lost or broken – someone's pride perhaps!

THE FIVE OF DISKS – WORRY – VENUS IN TAURUS

A young man kisses the hand of a lady: an illicit affair in the making. Venus signifies the affairs of the heart, and Taurus as the bull of earth brings a potent sensuality. But desire will topple the balance. The central card depicts the chariot of Mars, the opposite of Venus, as the wrecker of happiness. The five coins reveal the disorder caused by an excess of each of the elements.

Divinatory Significance

Misfortune, worry, disorder, possibly unemployment or laying off, loss of income and sudden change of expectation. Here is much uncertainty and anxiety, a feeling of being left out. Health issues may be relevant, too.

Scapini Five of Disks

ABOVE: *The game of "find the coin" relies on illusion and players must be wary; similarly the Five of Swords warns of underhanded dealing.*

Scapini Five of Swords

Reversed

There is light at the end of the tunnel. Something or someone has restored your faith in human nature and yourself.

THE FIVE OF WANDS – STRIFE – SATURN IN LEO

Men engage in a furious struggle using huge clubs as weapons. Saturn is the principle of restriction. Leo is just the opposite – open and expansive. Here is a battle royal between two powerful and conflicting desires, but a stalemate is likely to be the result.

Divinatory Significance

Struggle and argument. Rivals engage in power games; opinions are divided. Delays or misunderstandings are likely. A sense of challenge.

Reversed

The battle is over. A shift or reorganization has broken the log jam.

THE FIVE OF CUPS – DISAPPOINTMENT – MARS IN SCORPIO

A dying man dictates his will, surrounded by attendants. Who is disappointed here – the dying man who reviews his life, or the courtiers who will probably receive nothing from his inheritance? Scorpio is the sign of life and death. Mars represents the physical vitality of life – here the energy of Mars is being sapped. Was it used well in life? We cannot know.

Divinatory Significance

Loss, regret, friendship without meaning, marriage without love. Disappointment, grieving for what might have been and for what has been lost.

Reversed

Reunion. Time heals. Nurture the spark of hope and set out again.

Scapini Five of Wands

Scapini Five of Cups

95

The Sixes

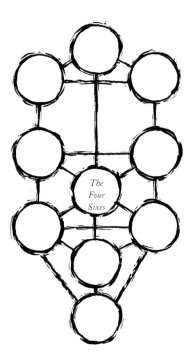

THE FOUR SIXES ON THE TREE OF LIFE

After the disharmony associated with the Fives, we now move to a place of complete harmony. If you look at the position of the sixth Sephirah, you will see that it stands exactly in the middle of the Tree. It brings the qualities of balance to all the Sixes. Furthermore, the title of this Sephirah – Tiphareth – means "Beauty." As a result, all of the sixes bring a positive quality of blessing in their respective suits. We will look at the Sixes in the Santa Fe Tarot.

THE SIX OF DISKS – SUCCESS – MOON IN TAURUS

This is a card of success. According to astrology, the moon is "exalted in Taurus" – in the most beneficial place. The emotional depths of the moon are satisfied by the nurturing stability of Taurus. A buffalo Yei travels into the mountains where there are four black tipis with earth circles instead of doorways. The buffalo Yei carries the remaining two earth disks.

Divinatory Significance

Here is a picture of success. It is a time for reaping financial rewards – investments, payouts, and dividends have multiplied. A time to pay off debts and repay favors. A time to share with others. You can afford to be charitable.

Reversed

An expected and deserved bonus does not appear. Bad debts loom; present prosperity is threatened. A selfish use of resources.

THE SIX OF SWORDS – SCIENCE – MERCURY IN AQUARIUS

Both Mercury and Aquarius are related to the mind. The substance mercury is a metaphorical image for thought processes, as it separates and reforms. Aquarius is symbolized by the water carrier, who pours out the waters of a higher consciousness. The card shows us two female Yeis together. Six spears of lightning shoot from their hands. Curved lightning supports the smaller of the two, but if the card were reversed, she would seem vulnerable. Her lightning would point toward the ground, where it would be dulled.

Six of Buffalo

Santa Fe Six of Disks

LEFT: *The Six of Wands represents victory after much effort, like the athlete who has trained hard for a race and then won it.*

Divinatory Significance

Here is movement (mental or physical), away from the past to new possibilities. A new attitude or new location will cause difficulties to fade.

Reversed

You cannot move away either mentally or physically. Stalemate.

Six of Lightning

Santa Fe Six of Swords

THE SIX OF WANDS – VICTORY – JUPITER IN LEO

Once again the title gives us the clue that we need. This is a card of victory. Jupiter and Leo are both victorious and expansive. Tiphareth is balancing and brings beauty. The result of all these good influences can only be positive. A female Yei holds six prayer sticks, two in her hands and four in her headdress. A rainbow bar protects her from behind.

Divinatory Significance

Here is victory – a well-earned success, a triumphant return or successful outcome to a dispute or negotiation. Friends are helpful; desires are realized.

Reversed

Inconclusive gain or an indefinite delay. Take care – the victory that you have expected may go elsewhere.

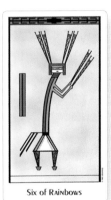

Six of Rainbows

Santa Fe Six of Wands

THE SIX OF CUPS – PLEASURE – SUN IN SCORPIO

Scorpio represents the deep waters within us. The card shows two brothers. It is often linked with nostalgia and memories of the past.

DIVINATORY SIGNIFICANCE

The pleasure of memory and the celebration of significant events. A spark from the past might flicker into new life, such as the renewal of a friendship.

Reversed

Let go of the past and move into the present. A time to get a perspective on childhood memories. Look to the future.

Six of Water

Santa Fe Six of Cups

ABOVE: *Disks represent practical-ity. Therefore the Seven of Disks can clash with the emotional aspect of the seventh Sephirah.*

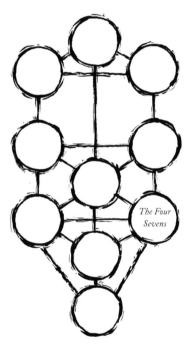

The Four Sevens

ABOVE: *The Sevens lie on Netzach (Victory), an area of the Tree of Life connected with the imagination and the emotions.*

The Sevens

THE FOUR SEVENS ON THE TREE OF LIFE

Contemporary Tarot often provides helpful visual clues for the Minor Arcana, but the historical packs are much less informative. The Marseilles Tarot, for example, merely presents the most basic imagery. The symbolism of the Tree of Life can be helpful for additional insight. The seventh Sephirah is connected with the imagination and the emotions, creating tension in relation to the intellectual and practical demands of the Swords and Disks. We will look at the Sevens in the Marseilles Tarot.

THE SEVEN OF DISKS – FAILURE – SATURN IN TAURUS

The clash of energies mentioned above results in failure. Taurus represents our ability to be productive in a practical way, but Saturn signifies the principle of limitation. Earthly success will be blighted.

Divinatory Significance

A transaction that goes wrong, disappointment, failure to secure desired results, unprofitable speculation, throwing good money after bad.

Reversed

Your commitments have become a burden; there are worries about mortgages or financial repayments. A general disillusionment with life.

THE SEVEN OF SWORDS – FUTILITY – MOON IN GEMINI

The Marseilles Tarot just shows seven swords. To acquire more information, we may profitably apply the astrological and Hermetic insights of the 20TH century to this historical pack. The title takes us into the essence of the card. The astrological signature completes the picture. The emotional needs represented by the moon will feel ill-at-ease in the airy mental realm of Gemini.

Divinatory Significance

Uncertainty, vacillation, a failure of nerve, perhaps stealth and trickery. You may have placed hopes in a sterile situation or untrustworthy person.

Marseilles Seven of Disks   *Marseilles Seven of Swords*   *Marseilles Seven of Wands*   *Marseilles Seven of Cups*

Reversed

The situation has been righted with an apology or an admission of fault. Back on track, your goals seem clearer.

THE SEVEN OF WANDS – VALOR – MARS IN LEO

Once again, the astrological signature is our guide. Mars and Leo support each other with a dynamic energy. The card is called Valor, which combines both qualities. It describes the quality required in the moment.

Divinatory Significance

You will need to be valiant to defend your position with strength and determination, justifying your beliefs and values. Someone wants to pick a fight with you. You feel embattled, but you have the courage to deal with this.

Reversed

The immediate situation is diffused. Tension exists but does not surface. An uneasy and probably temporary solution.

THE SEVEN OF CUPS – DEBAUCHERY – VENUS IN SCORPIO

Venus represents our desire to love. Scorpio takes us into the deepest recesses of ourselves. Together these qualities make for intensity and self-indulgence, debauchery and excess.

Divinatory Significance

Everything seems tempting, and you are pulled in different directions. Your desires can lead you into excess and lack of self-control – you are spoiled for choice. This is not a good time to make a decision. Your mind is befuddled.

Reversed

Clarity has dawned, the clouds part; you can see the way ahead.

ABOVE: *The intensity and self-indulgence of Scorpio and Venus slip into debauchery when they meet with the emotions of the suit of Cups.*

The Eights

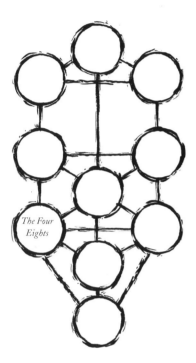

The Four Eights

ABOVE: *The eighth Sephirah is Hod (Splendor). It relates to the splendor of the mind.*

THE EIGHTS ON THE TREE OF LIFE

We will look at the Eights in the Golden Dawn Tarot. The Order of the Golden Dawn did much to cement the Tree of Life and the Tarot together, but their Minor Arcana provides only modest information. Students of the Order were expected to know the subtle connections with the Tree of Life, so only minimal information was presented.

THE EIGHT OF DISKS – PRUDENCE – SUN IN VIRGO

The astrological signature provides information. The sign of Virgo represents industry, service, and practical skills. Virgoans are noted for meticulous attention to detail and a careful approach to work. This card is called Prudence, a very Virgoan characteristic.

Divinatory Significance

Hard work brings a reward. Good fortune in money matters. A determination to improve your chances through practical steps – perhaps learning a new skill or seeking new qualifications.

Reversed

Maybe a wish to short-circuit the system by quick and even underhanded methods. Gambling or unwise speculation.

THE EIGHT OF SWORDS – INTERFERENCE – JUPITER IN GEMINI

Jupiter brings expansion to the mental realm of Gemini. However, its effect is to expand a sense of the trivial and bring about a real diminution of mental horizons. Excessive attention to trivia brings interference, not splendor.

Divinatory Significance

The mental anguish of feeling trapped by a situation, person, or circumstances. Don't be petty-minded. There is a tendency to fuss over the insignificant while missing the importance of the bigger picture.

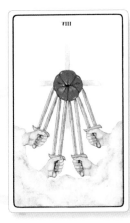

Golden Dawn Eight of Swords

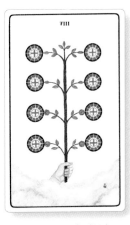

Golden Dawn Eight of Disks

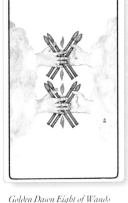

Golden Dawn Eight of Wands

Reversed

A great desire to be free, escaping through your own ideas and initiative.

THE EIGHT OF WANDS – SWIFTNESS – MERCURY IN SAGITTARIUS

We simply see two bundles of wands, one above the other, held in two sets of hands. Both Mercury and Sagittarius imply qualities of mental speed. Mercury is the quicksilver of the mind, and Sagittarius is the questing spirit that takes off in any direction.

Divinatory Significance

The action around you is fast-moving and skillful. Your ideas will rapidly become real. Success, skill, and travel are indicated.

Reversed

Your ideas may fall flat before reaching their intended mark.

THE EIGHT OF CUPS – INDOLENCE – SATURN IN PISCES

The sign of Pisces is related to water, creative inspiration, and even psychic abilities, but here it is afflicted by the restrictive and dour limitations of Saturn. The result is a depressing feeling that nothing is worth doing.

Divinatory Significance

A decline of interest, a loss of appetite for life, dissatisfaction, depression. Life feels empty and without meaning. Perhaps it is time to look for something more meaningful.

Reversed

Walking away can create new possibilities. Involvement in meaningful activity is close at hand.

Golden Dawn Eight of Cups

ABOVE: *The Eight of Cups is linked to Pisces (top) and Saturn (bottom). Pisces is related to creativity; Saturn is a restrictive influence.*

The Nines

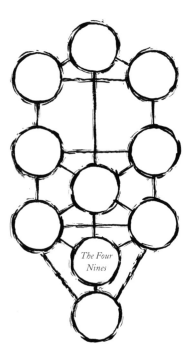

ABOVE: *The Nines are placed on Yesod (Foundation). This position is related to the unconscious.*

The Four Nines

THE FOUR NINES ON THE TREE OF LIFE

The Nines are related to the ninth Sephirah, Yesod, which means Foundation. This Sephirah is also related to the unconscious realm as a foundation. Yesod is situated in an essentially balanced and stable position beneath the beneficial influence of the sixth Sephirah. We will look at the Nines in the Egyptian Tarot.

THE NINE OF DISKS – GAIN – VENUS IN VIRGO

We see nine different coins in three columns. The title, together with the astrological signature and the image, are unanimous in proclaiming a gain, most probably of a financial nature. Venus is our joy. As one of the earth signs, Virgo represents the place of our application. The result of these two energies is a deserved gain.

Divinatory Significance

A financial gain as the result of careful planning, hard work, and industrious application. If a legacy comes your way, it is because someone has thought you trustworthy enough to husband it.

Reversed

Foolish moves. Rash decisions and lack of foresight in the past now bring the only possible harvest: a negative one.

THE NINE OF SWORDS – CRUELTY – MARS IN GEMINI

The suit of the mind is not at ease in the Sephirah of Yesod and its emotional characteristics. The result is turmoil. The card shows us nine swords in neat array. The rest of the story lies in the title and astrological signature. Mars is the physical power that drives the sword home. Gemini is the sphere of the mind. The results can only be cruelty and torment.

Divinatory Significance

Mental torture, despair, waking in the night from tormented sleep. All around seems dark. Is there no escape? A possibility of health issues.

LEFT: *A reversed Nine of Swords shows that light will penetrate darkness, bringing an end to problems.*

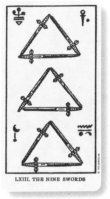

Egyptian Nine of Disks

Reversed

There is light at the end of the tunnel, remember that nothing lasts forever.

THE NINE OF WANDS – STRENGTH – MOON IN SAGITTARIUS

Yesod is called the Foundation, which implies the strength to endure and stand firm. We see nine wands or scepters arranged in three triangles. The astrological signature presents us with two opposing qualities. The lunar qualities seek comfort, but the Sagittarian qualities relish excitement. If there is an affray, you will join in and love every minute of it.

Egyptian Nine of Swords

Divinatory Significance

You have good inner reserves and strength of character, but these are being called on. Who is draining your strength? Be mindful of health problems.

Reversed

The battle has been won. Vigilance is still required, but the real action is over.

THE NINE OF CUPS – HAPPINESS – JUPITER IN PISCES

Nine cups are arranged in three triangles. Once more the title and astrological signature tell us all we need to know. The sign of Pisces with all its sensitivity and capacity for human warmth is expanded by the gregarious Jupiter. In fact, Jupiter is said to be exalted in the sign of Pisces; in other words, here is the perfect marriage. The result, of course, is happiness.

Egyptian Nine of Wands

Divinatory Significance

Contentment, relaxation, and ease. This is the time for socializing and enjoyment. Life is good at the moment. A time to count one's blessings.

Reversed

The temptations of ease and success are beckoning. Take care: for indulgence feels good only in the short run.

Egyptian Nine of Cups

The Tens

Motherpeace Ten of Disks

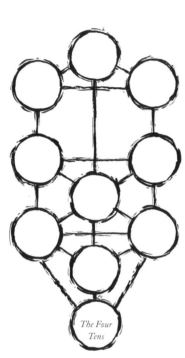

The Four Tens

ABOVE: *The Tens are sited on Malkuth (Kingdom), part of the Tree of Life where Disks and Cups find a natural home.*

BELOW: *The Ten of Disks can indicate similarly shaped rewards: piles of money!*

THE FOUR TENS ON THE TREE OF LIFE

The Tens are assigned to the tenth Sephirah, Malkuth, which is called the Kingdom. The suits of Disks and Cups have a natural affinity here, but spirit and mind being more abstract qualities, they may succumb to a sense of restriction. Our last look at the various Tarot decks compares four different styles. This may help you to decide which style you favor.

THE TEN OF DISKS – WEALTH – MERCURY IN VIRGO

The Motherpeace Tarot shows a ceremonial gathering. Women greet a new mother and her baby. This is the recognition of a change from one stage of life to another – a rite of passage to celebrate the transition.

Divinatory Significance

A crowning in the kingdom, stability, money, security, and success – reaping the rewards of much hard work. Perhaps a pensions payment or salary increase. Also the possibility of a positive transition from single to married, or from employment to retirement.

Reversed

Security is in doubt or a reputation is in jeopardy. Business matters are fraught with problems. Big financial decisions are unstable. It feels as if circumstances are conspiring against you.

THE TEN OF SWORDS – RUIN – SUN IN GEMINI

In the Russian Tarot we see a man lying dead, pierced by ten swords. What did he do to deserve this end? The image alone is perfectly clear; there is no need for any additional information. The title sums up what we already know – ruin has descended.

Divinatory Significance

Defeat and catastrophe. The end has arrived; the battle has sadly been lost. It is a stab in the back.

Russian Ten of Swords   *Santa Fe Ten of Wands*   *Zolar Ten of Cups*

Reversed

In every ending there is new beginning. It is time to totally re-evaluate what you have been trying to accomplish. Lick your wounds, look to the future.

THE TEN OF WANDS – OPPRESSION – SATURN IN SAGITTARIUS

The Santa Fe Tarot shows a rainbow Yei with slightly bowed head. He carries five blue prayer sticks in each hand, but they have become heavy and burdensome. The astrological signature shows that the heaviness of Saturn has overcome the joyous freedom of the Sagittarian spirit, which is oppressed within the limitations of the material world.

Divinatory Significance

A man is weighed down with the responsibilities and burdens that he has to shoulder. Try to delegate or share the weight with others.

Reversed

The weight of the burden has become too much to carry alone. Give up some responsibilities or they may break you. Health problems may be indicated.

THE TEN OF CUPS – SATIETY – MARS IN PISCES

The Zolar Tarot gives a simple, even naive, view of emotional fulfillment. Here is the assembled family and the rainbow of cups. Is this still a picture of domestic perfection? A word of care – Mars brings a restless energy to Pisces. The card is called Satiety, which is saturation!

Divinatory Significance

Contentment and real harmony. The fulfillment of the human dream for happiness and joy in relationships. The rainbow signifies hope for tomorrow.

Reversed

The situation will not last. Happiness is fleeting.

ABOVE: *In Greek mythology, the burly Atlas was believed to hold up the heavens: a real weight to shoulder.*

Fire

Wands

Leo *Sagittarius* *Aries*

Air

Swords

Aquarius *Gemini* *Libra*

Water

Cups

Scorpio *Pisces* *Cancer*

Earth

Disks

Taurus *Virgo* *Capricorn*

The Court Cards

THE ROYAL FAMILY

It is no surprise to find court cards in a system that originated at court. Medieval court life revolved around the king, who exercised supreme power. The queen was also a person of great importance, and knights and pages were characters in the medieval world of chivalry, romance and courtly life. There are some variations on this theme, but the basic model gives us 16 characters: King, Queen, Page, and Knight in each of the four suits. The four suits can be thought of as separate courts, each with its own nature:

ABOVE: *The Motherpeace Tarot has replaced some of the traditional medieval characters with characters representing spiritual practice.*

The Courts

- The Court of Wands is associated with the element of fire and the astrological signs of Leo, Sagittarius, and Aries.
- The Court of Swords is associated with element of air and the astrological signs of Aquarius, Gemini, and Libra.
- The Court of Cups is associated with the element of water and the astrological signs of Scorpio, Pisces, and Cancer.
- The Court of Disks is associated with the element of earth and the astrological signs of Taurus, Virgo, and Capricorn.

MODERN TAROT

Modern Tarot has moved away from a medieval setting. In the Motherpeace Tarot, the King is called the Shaman, the Queen is the Priestess, and the Knight and Page are the Son and Daughter. The Shaman and the Priestess are servants of wisdom, not of the state. The Son and the Daughter represent the junior powers of the suit.

In the Medicine Woman Tarot, the King, Queen, Knight, and Page are replaced by the Exemplar, the Power Lodge, the Totem, and the Apprentice. Despite the new language, there is still the continuity of ideas. The Exemplar, King, and Shaman express the developed and mature qualities of the suit; the Power Lodge, Queen and

Key Words - Cups

Feelings, depth, emotion, sensitivity, relationship, compassion, caring, love, comfort, friendship, companionship, colleagues, creative activities, fulfillment, celebration, desolation, romance, surprise.

Key Words - Disks

Fertility, bank balance, property, business, money, outgoings, security, increment, growth, status, practical application, manufacture, craftsmanship, construction, using natural resources.

Key Words - Swords

Ideas, worries, serious decisions, delays, disappointments, losses, separations, travel, movement, ambition, enthusiasm, excitement, courage, enterprise, restlessness, impulsiveness, recklessness.

Key Words - Wands

Energy, enthusiasm, communications, letters, phone calls, distant travel, enterprise, business concerns, negotiations.

Priestess represent its supportive and empowering qualities. The totem, son, and knight express the more youthful and less developed qualities of the suit, as do the daughter, page, and apprentice.

Although it seems natural to think of this archetypal family as the father and mother, and the son and daughter, the Golden Dawn Tarot chose to swap the roles otherwise assigned to the King and the Knight. The Thoth Tarot develops this further, so that each pack contains a Knight and Queen, a Page and a Princess, but no King, which can be confusing.

ABOVE: *In a reading, Kings may represent mature men, father figures, bosses, or men over 35.*

WHO THE CARDS REPRESENT

The Court cards represent either other people in the Seeker's life or an aspect of the person having a reading. To determine which is the case, ask the Seeker if the question concerns other people, and make a judgment accordingly. When the court cards represent other people, the following guidelines are usually observed:

- The Kings represent mature men, father figures, male bosses over 35.
- The Queens represent mature women, mothers, female bosses.
- The Knights represent younger men, husbands, lovers, and brothers.
- The Pages represent teenagers, youths, students, trainees.

When the characters represent parts and qualities of yourself:

- The Kings represent the mature, qualified, experienced qualities of character – for example, the King of Wands represents your developed qualities of enterprise, command, and skill.
- The Queen represents your established qualities of character – for example, the Queen of Cups represents your well-developed compassionate and loving nature.
- The Knight represents your dynamic and still-changing qualities – for example, the Knight of Swords represents your active enthusiasm in a new area of mental activity.
- The Page represent all that is youthful, inexperienced, untried within you – for example, the Page of Disks represents a new departure in an area of commerce or industry.

ABOVE: *The characters of court life are metaphors for people in your own life. They can also represent your personality traits.*

Marseilles King of Disks

Marseilles King of Swords

Marseilles King of Wands

Marseilles King of Cups

The Four Kings

THE CHARACTER OF THE KING

The Four Kings represent mature and established men, authority figures, and experts in specialized fields; in other words, men who are experienced in life. We will look at the Four Kings from the Marseilles Tarot.

THE KING OF DISKS

In the Marseilles Tarot this card is called the King of Deniers. There is nothing to show that he is a king, and his crown is hidden by a large hat. He holds a large gold coin in one hand, so he could be a merchant rather than a ruler. The coin represents the wealth of the state.

Divinatory Significance

This is a man who is down-to-earth and practical, with tangible achievements to show for his industry. He enjoys the good life and its pleasures. He is generous, with a flair for business.

Reversed

When reversed, this character is greedy and avaricious. He is very conscious of money, financial security, and worldly success.

THE KING OF SWORDS

The King of Swords sits on a block. He wears moon epaulets and holds the sword directly upright in a neutral position. The sword is unsheathed and ready for use if necessary, but this is just a watchful defense. Apart from its martial connotations, the sword represents the freedom of the mind. During the Renaissance, many of the independent courts throughout Europe became centers of great learning and intellectual freedom.

Divinatory Significance

This king is a decision-maker, a person of authority who makes good use of mental skills to create a professional path in life. He is a diplomatic and trustworthy person, a good arbitrator, intelligent, always learning, open to new ideas and views, a good negotiator and a reliable witness.

Reversed

This shows confused thinking and prejudice. Here is a manipulative person who enjoys combative encounters.

THE KING OF WANDS

In the Marseilles Tarot this character is called the King of Staffs. The staff represents the power of the state to achieve its goals. The independent city states of medieval Europe had much freedom of action and movement; the staff of state had the power to bring things to pass.

ABOVE: *A reversed King of Swords reveals a person who manipulates others, and enjoys locking horns in antagonistic encounters.*

Divinatory Significance

This man is a successful and determined hard worker, warm and good-humored, loyal, honest, and generous.

Reversed

When reversed, we see all the characteristics of poor kingship. He is ambitious, demanding, and driven by the need for success. He enjoys controlling others and uses all the resources at his disposal to be self-serving.

THE KING OF CUPS

Here is an aged king with a sorrowful expression. Is he offering the large chalice to the viewer, or is it for himself? Is he drowning his own sorrows in a melancholy bout of introspection? He is, after all, the King of Cups.

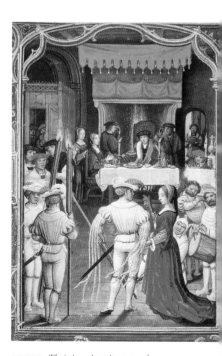

Divinatory Significance

This king offers a deep understanding of the human condition. He is a good friend, a wise counsel, and a guiding hand. He understands the sadness of the human condition because he has witnessed it all at first hand.

Reversed

When reversed, this king shows immaturity, inexperience, and insincerity. He has not drunk deeply enough of the cup of life to understand its bittersweet nature. He is insubstantial, untrustworthy, and shallow.

ABOVE: *The independent city states of medieval Europe had access to considerable resources, enabling them to flourish.*

Thoth Queen of Disks

The Four Queens

THE CHARACTER OF THE QUEEN

The Four Queens bring a mature experience of life and a well-rounded viewpoint. We will look at the Four Queens in the Thoth Tarot.

THE QUEEN OF DISKS

She is found in the kingdom of nature, wearing huge horns. Her scepter is topped by the cube of earth. The goat represents the earth sign of Capricorn.

Divinatory Significance

This figure is inspired by nature. She is creative, practical, trustworthy, responsible, sympathetic, organized, efficient, generous, and pleasure loving.

Reversed

When reversed, her talents are unused, and her creativity is undeveloped. She lacks confidence and security, relying on others to make her decisions. She is afraid of responsibilities and broods over lost opportunities.

THE QUEEN OF SWORDS

Her kingdom is that of the mind and imagination. Is the severed head the latest victim of her razor-sharp mind?

Divinatory significance

She is educated, outspoken, independent, mentally sharp, and clear thinking. She is direct in word and deed, and values her liberty and freedom. She is respected for her unbiased opinion and fair judgment.

ABOVE: *Dionysus, the god of ecstasy and wild inspiration, carries a cone-topped wand called the thyrsus. The Queen of Wands carries an identical wand.*

BELOW: *The Queen of Disks is part of the kingdom of nature. Her colors are the greens and browns of the fertile earth.*

Thoth Queen of Swords

Thoth Queen of Wands

Thoth Queen of Cups

Reversed

When reversed, we find a sharp tongue and a love of gossip. This is not a person to be trusted with confidences. She loves intrigue and bears grudges. She broods on the past and is self-opinionated and small-minded.

THE QUEEN OF WANDS

Here is a wonderful and powerful evocation of the forces of elemental fire. She burns with passion, power and creativity.

Divinatory significance

This queen is enthusiastic, energetic, outspoken, and direct. She has a natural authority and gives counsel to all who seek advice. She relates to others with warmth, spontaneity and affection. She is creative, popular, and confident.

Reversed

When reversed, this queen is ambitious, selfish, domineering, and temperamental. She is respected, but not popular; quick-tempered and self-serving. She is openly ambitious and driven by a restless desire for personal success.

THE QUEEN OF CUPS

The Queen is veiled by swirling curves of endless light, her image reflected in the water. Her appearance is designed to evoke the qualities of dreaminess and illusion associated with the water signs.

ABOVE: *The lotus flower is clasped by the Queen of Cups. It signifies spiritual awakening.*

Divinatory significance

She is creative, inspired, artistic and expressive, helpful and supportive to others. She offers a loving sensitivity and a compassionate nature.

Reversed

Oversensitized to the world and its pain. Has escapist wishes and self-sacrificing tendencies. Soft-hearted, dreamy, and overwhelmed by all feelings.

The Four Knights

THE CHARACTER OF THE KNIGHT

The Four Knights represent an outgoing, questing energy. They symbolize openness to new experience. As mounted and equipped riders, the knights can represent messages or communication. We will look at the knights in the Motherpeace Tarot, where we will meet them as sons of the various suits.

THE SON OF DISKS

We meet the Son of Disks in the greenwood, where he is perfecting his skills. Everything around him is green, suggesting fertile growth. There is a robin and a dragonfly. We are reminded of the mythology of Robin Hood.

Divinatory Significance

This character is hard-working, practical, dependable, and patient. He is ready to develop and improve his skills. He is conscientious and steadfast.

Reversed

When reversed, we find a lack of application and staying power. His skills are not fully honed, and he lacks the determination for self-improvement. His goals in life are still uncertain.

THE SON OF SWORDS

We meet the Son of Swords strolling on an empty plain. Broken flowers strew the ground. The figure is naked except for a cloak and the helmet of an ancient warrior. He is armed with a sword and a quiver of arrows, and carries a dead dove in one hand. He seems rather like a restless adventurer looking for the next opportunity. He already sees the next prize on the horizon: it has attracted his attention, and we know that he will set out to achieve it.

Divinatory Significance

Here is a restless wanderer, an opportunist with many strings to his bow. He undertakes many plans and projects. He brings a destructive quality to everything he does, because his actions and the consequences have become separated. He is very persuasive.

ABOVE: *Alexander the Great is the embodiment of the energetic, questing character of the Knights.*

LEFT: *The Son of Wands is a great performer, revelling in the appreciation of a crowd.*

Motherpeace Son of Disks

Reversed

His destructive traits are softened in this position. He is more able to consider the opinions of others, to value creative and artistic activities, and to offer support for the initiative shown by others.

THE SON OF WANDS

We meet the Son of Wands dressed up and performing a ritual for his community. We sense his vitality and unrestrained energy. He loves to be the center of attention. He enjoys relating to a crowd of people.

Divinatory Significance

This person is larger than life. He loves company and likes to talk and entertain. He has many interests and projects, which he supports with enthusiasm and energy. He hates to be bored and loves fun.

Reversed

This character would like to be the center of attention, but lacks a natural rapport with others. He contrives to be noticed by being controversial, challenging, and confrontational. He is quick-tempered and demanding.

THE SON OF CUPS

The Son of Cups sits comfortably in the yoga lotus position. He seems self-absorbed and contented. His world is encompassed within an ovoid. Beyond his immediate vicinity we see the color lavender and the datura plant.

Divinatory Significance

This figure is always sensitive to others. He is compassionate, kind, idealistic, and supports good causes. He loves music and dance, the theater, and art. He needs to express what he feels and will always find a way to do this.

Reversed

When reversed, he is caught in a world of his own. His creativity is blocked and he needs to rediscover it or he will be frustrated and unhappy.

Motherpeace Son of Swords

Motherpeace Son of Wands

Motherpeace Son of Cups

The Four Pages

THE CHARACTER OF THE PAGE

The Four Pages bring the freshness of youthful enthusiasm. As the youngest member of the family of court cards, the Page can represent children or young people. We will look at the Page in the Zolar Tarot.

THE PAGE OF DISKS

We meet a young man in medieval guise, standing alone in a landscape. He lifts a disk inscribed with a star – the pentacle. The disk may be thought of as our environment. It is a symbol of spirit presence incarnate within the material world. The disk seems to be the focus of the young man's attention – perhaps he contemplates its meaning or offers it to the viewer.

Divinatory Significance

Here is the perpetual student with an openness to all life's experience. He is willing to learn from everything and everyone, and is eager for advice and practical help. He is willing to work hard, is creative and expressive, and enjoys natural things inspired by the natural world.

Reversed

When reversed, this represents an unbending trait. This person is unwilling to take advice from others. Young and headstrong, and not interested in what others have to teach, he is determined to go his own way.

THE PAGE OF SWORDS

The Page of Swords stands outside, swinging his sword through the air. He wears the clothes typical of a medieval page. It is a windy day, and the branches of the trees sway in the wind. Clouds move rapidly across the sky.

Divinatory Significance

The Page of Swords has a youthful vitality, with a fresh and open approach to life. He seeks excitement and is easily bored. He likes a challenge and is excited by the possibilities of new developments. He is versatile and well-informed. He has many interests and an adaptable mind. He learns quickly.

ABOVE: *The Page of Swords is fired up by a challenge and is always looking for new excitements to keep boredom at bay.*

A very dark-haired, dark-eyed boy or girl. Brings pleasant news.

J ♦

MINOR ARCANA

THE PAGE OF PENTACLES

Unlucky speculations, Disappointments, losses in friendships. May hear some bad news.

Zolar Page of Disks

A dark-haired boy or girl. Betrayal of a friend. Rivalry in love.

J ♠

MINOR ARCANA

THE PAGE OF SWORDS

Vindication and victory over a rival.

Zolar Page of Swords

Blonde, blue-eyed young man or girl. Good news. If next to Queen of Pentacles, a brilliant marriage.

J ♣

MINOR ARCANA

THE PAGE OF WANDS

Unpleasant news. Doubtful success of an undertaking.

Zolar Page of Wands

A young man or girl with light brown hair and hazel eyes. News or message about the birth of a child.

J ♥

MINOR ARCANA

THE PAGE OF CUPS

Secret or deceptive undertakings will soon be discovered.

Zolar Page of Cups

Reversed

When reversed, the sword becomes a weapon. This person is more than capable of defending himself. The mind is sharp, unpredictable, and fickle. He is amusing in a cynical and clever way, but beneath the surface there is little substance. This Page of Swords is a master of words.

THE PAGE OF WANDS

The Page of Wands stands alone outside, holding a staff cut from living wood. It has sprouted new leaves, and he is intently looking at these.

Divinatory Significance

The Page of Wands has the power to motivate and inspire, capable of revitalizing a project or bringing a new idea to life. He is idealistic, keen, and able. This Page of Wands loves nothing more than an impossible challenge.

Reversed

When reversed, this page manufactures his own excitement. He loves the thrill of danger and the lure of the impossible.

THE PAGE OF CUPS

This page offers us a cup. It is a curious cup, with a fish peeping over the top.

Divinatory Significance

The Page of Cups likes to amuse and delight. He has an open heart and a warm spirit. He is an easy companion and is genuinely charming. He enjoys simple things. He is naturally kind, compassionate, sensitive, and intuitive.

Reversed

He seeks illusion and escape, and is prone to fantasy and unrealistic hopes. He often seeks the short-lived high and the momentary escape, which he finds preferable to real interchange and emotional involvement.

ABOVE: *A reversed Page of Wands reveals someone who has a love of danger and physical thrills. He is always keen to tell everyone about his exciting exploits.*

Divination

READING PICTURES

The Tarot is probably the most popular form of Western divination, and the basic principles can be learned quite easily. Laying a Tarot spread might be thought of as holding a mirror to life – it reveals a picture that we can see and reflect upon. Laying out a spread can be as simple or as complicated as you wish. Some people like to burn incense or light a candle. These are simply ways of retaining a spiritual focus.

All Tarot spreads are blueprints. Each placement in the spread defines a certain area of life, and the cards are then read in conjunction with the assigned place. For instance, should the Fool appear in a position connected with work, it might indicate a new career move. If the Fool appears in a position related to the emotions, it might indicate suddenly falling in love.

WARMING UP

The idea of combining many cards together can seem a bit daunting, so let us see how the principles of divination can be built up.

It is common to first select a significator card to represent the Questioner or Seeker. This can be done in two ways. Either you must decide, at the onset, which one of the court cards best represents you, or you must choose a card at random and let it represent you. Which approach do you prefer? Once you have made a choice, use it whenever you prepare a spread. Take a single card on a daily basis and keep notes. Do this same cards reappear? You will soon feel the need for supporting information from other cards.

CREATING A SPREAD

When you are ready to try a spread with several cards, just do it and see what happens. To create a spread, use the following stages:

1 Opening Yourself

Spend a few moments attuning yourself. Gently withdraw into your own inner space. Enter a receptive and meditative state of mind. Open yourself to your own spiritual guidance.

ABOVE RIGHT: *Some people like to use a square of silk to lay the spread on, or to burn incense or light a candle during a reading.*

BELOW: *The soft glow of candle-light helps to create a conducive atmosphere and a link with the spiritual.*

LEFT: *First, a card is chosen to represent the Seeker and taken out of the pack. The Seeker then shuffles the deck while considering the question to be asked.*

2 Choosing a Significator

Choose a card to represent the Seeker. This can be done either by matching one of the court cards to the person or by allowing a random choice to serve. Take this out of the pack. It can be laid as part of the spread, if directed, or placed to one side.

3 The Question

Ask the Seeker to frame the question clearly. The question may be kept private or disclosed. It should cover only one topic. A vague question will elicit vague answers.

4 The Shuffle

The significator card is not included in this. The Seeker is given the deck to shuffle and is asked to think about the question while shuffling. When the pack is shuffled, the Seeker is asked to cut the pack into three piles, which are placed face down. Next, the piles are recombined in any order into one deck by the Seeker and finally handed back to you, the Reader.

6 The Spread

Lay out the cards according to the blueprint of the spread you have chosen. When you are still learning, make a note of the spread for further reflection.

ABOVE: *After shuffling the deck, the Seeker must cut it into three piles, placed face down.*

7 Interpreting the Spread

The Tarot mirror has been unveiled. The spread has been laid. There is no shortcut to successful reading. It is a finely balanced art between your intuition and your understanding of the cards. However, the only way to develop both is practice, practice, and more practice. Make notes and see how cards and life's circumstances correlate.

ABOVE: *How to lay out a five-card spread.*

BELOW: *The Four Directions.*

Spreads Old and New

THE FOUR DIRECTIONS

Imagine yourself standing with arms outstretched to the left and right. See yourself at the center of four directions. East is ahead, west is behind, north is on your left, south is on your right. Where does the future lie? Where does the past lie? Instinctively we feel that the future lies ahead and the past lies behind. What lies upon your left and right hand? The left has always represented the unconscious. The right has always represented consciousness. Now let us translate the four directions into a spread.

Choose a significator and place it at the center. Place the remaining cards clockwise, starting in the west. The completed pattern can now be read as follows: where the person stands, has been, is going; forces from the unconscious and consciousness. This five-card spread takes us toward the Celtic Cross spread, which includes ten cards.

East
Ahead: the future

North
Left: the unconscious

South
Right: consciousness

West
Behind: the past

The Four Directions

CARD 1
Significator – Where I stand

CARD 2 – *The West*
The past – Where I have been

CARD 3 – *The North*
Forces uprising from the unconscious

CARD 4 – *The East*
The future – Where I am going

CARD 5 – *The South*
Forces appearing in consciousness

THE CELTIC CROSS

This is perhaps the most popular and widely used of all Tarot spreads, but no one seems to know how it began. It is composed of two parts, which resemble the two parts of the standing cross so common throughout Ireland. The standing cross incorporates a circle and a cross together upon an upright. We have already created the circle and cross together through the spread of The Four Directions. This can be expanded into the traditional Celtic cross. Now we lay two cards at the central point. The second card crosses the first and represents obstacles in the present. We have already used the circle layout as a sphere in which we stand. Now we can build a vertical ladder, which represents the upright of the cross. It is laid to the right and represents the way we travel forward in life. It contains four cards.

Final Outcome

The Celtic Cross

5

Possible Future

9

Hopes and Fears

CARD 1

Starting point – the significator

CARD 2

Challenges in the present

CARD 3

That which is below – the past

CARD 4

*That which is surfacing
from the past*

CARD 5

*The way you are facing
the immediate present*

4

*Recent Event
(a couple of
months)*

1
2

*Helps and Hindrances
Present*

6

*Immediate
Future*

8

*1. Environment,
home, or work
2. How others see
you in the situation*

CARD 6

*That which is coming into
play in the near future*

CARD 7

Where you stand – how you see things

3

Past

7

*On your mind
Mental Outlook
How you see it*

CARD 8

How others see you

CARD 9

Hopes and fears

CARD 10

Fulfillment – outcome, the future

THE CIRCLE OF THE YEAR

The circular form seems very natural as a blueprint for a reading. Though time appears to be linear, at a deeper level it is also seasonal and cyclical so you may find a circular spread more satisfying. Some spreads lend themselves especially well to the passing of time. The 12 months of the year naturally suggest a twelve-card arrangement. If you don't feel confident about astrology, take 12 cards to represent the 12 months ahead in a straightforward correlation. Lay the significator in the center. However, if you are a confident astrologer, the 12 cards can be read in conjunction with astrological correspondences.

These spreads will provide the basis for plenty of experience. The spread of the Four Directions orientates you within the framework of the sacred circle. The meanings for each of the directions can be developed as you become more confident. The Circle of the Year provides considerable scope for honing your skills.

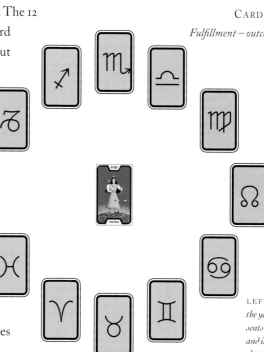

LEFT: *In the circle of
the year, each card represents an astrological sign
and its associated
characteristics.*

ABOVE: *Look to see which is the most common suit in the spread.*

ABOVE: *Assess the proportion of court cards in the spread.*

ABOVE: *Look at the cards and see whether any numbers are repeated.*

A Quick Guide to the Major Arcana

FINDING PATTERNS

Laying out the spread is the first step. Interpreting it is the second. Begin by looking for patterns and connections. Assess the following:

1 Which is the most common suit?

2 Which is the second most dominant suit?

3 Which suit is absent?

4 Are there any reversed cards?

5 What is the balance of court cards to the whole?

6 What is the balance of Minor Arcana cards to the whole?

7 What is the balance of Major Arcana cards to the whole?

8 Are any numbers repeated?

This analysis will provide a skeleton framework. Use the key points to flesh out your interpretation.

THE MAJOR ARCANA

The appearance of a disproportionate number of Major Arcana cards adds weight and significance to a reading, emphasizing that it is a time of importance for the Seeker.

Trump O, The Fool: A beginning, originality, spirituality, folly, and eccentricity in material matters

Trump I, The Magician: Constructive power, initiative, skill, activity, cleverness

Trump II, The High Priestess: Wisdom, fluctuation, secrecy, things hidden, deep issues, intuition

Trump III, The Empress: Fertility, fruitfulness, abundance, happiness, maternity

Trump IV, The Emperor: Stability, power, reason, control, authority, ambition

Trump V, The Hierophant: Revelation, the influence of organized religion, spiritual teachings

Trump VI, The Lovers: Love, partnership, personal relationships, marriage, inspiration

Fool, Magician, High Priestess

Empress, Emperor, Hierophant

Lovers, Chariot, Strength

Hermit, Wheel of Fortune, Justice

*Trump VII, **The Chariot:*** Triumph, victory, success, self assertion, travel

*Trump VIII, **Strength:*** Courage, spiritual strength, self mastery, fortitude

*Trump IX, **The Hermit:*** Wisdom, the lone pioneer, prudence, inner counsel, divine inspiration

*Trump X, **The Wheel of Fortune:*** The cycles of life, an unexpected turn, a change

*Trump XI, **Justice:*** Legal affairs, justice, a judgment, decision

*Trump XII, **The Hanged Man:*** Surrender, an act of sacrifice, unconventional behavior

*Trump XIII, **Death:*** The end of a phase, a new beginning, a transformation

*Trump XIV, **Temperance:*** Balance, partnership, good prospect

*Trump XV, **The Devil:*** Bondage, material desires, a trial, obsessions

*Trump XVI, **The Tower:*** Failure, the crash of expectations, re-evaluation, unfulfilled ambition

*Trump XVII, **The Star:*** A blessing, hope, insight, a gift, a promise

*Trump XVIII, **The Moon:*** Organic change, hidden currents, uncertainty, dissatisfaction

*Trump XIX, **The Sun:*** Enlightenment, joy, success, prosperity

*Trump XX, **Judgment:*** Decision, change of direction, final settlement, waking up

*Trump XXI, **The World:*** Completion of a cycle, success, achievement

Hanged Man, Death, Temperance

Devil, Tower, Star

Sun, Moon, Judgment, World

The Minor Arcana

THE SUIT OF SWORDS

An emphasis on ideas, decisions, the mind, communication often connected with conflict, matters that require a specialist, travel, movement, enterprise, plans.

THE SUIT OF DISKS

An emphasis on resources and values, property and possessions, growth, status, manufacture, construction, trade, career.

THE SUIT OF WANDS

An emphasis on energy, enthusiasm, communications, letters, phone calls, distant travel, enterprise, business concerns, negotiations.

THE SUIT OF CUPS

An emphasis on feelings, emotion, relationship, love, friendship, companionship, colleagues, fulfillment, celebration, romance.

THE COURT CARDS

An emphasis on people: *Kings:* Mature men, *Queens:* Mature women, *Knights:* Contemporaries, *Pages:* Children and young people.

ABOVE: *The four suits from the Thoth Tarot. Each suit has distinct connotations.*

The Thoth Prince

The Thoth Princess

The Thoth Knight

LEFT: *The Eight of Wands gives notice that a journey is on the cards.*

NUMBER PATTERNS

Repeated numbers give emphasis: see box opposite.

QUICK REFERENCE

Look out for the following shorthand:

Beginnings: The Wheel of Fortune, The Fool, The Star

Endings: The Tower, Death, The Wheel of Fortune, The World

Love and Romance: The Lovers, Ace of Cups, Two of Cups

Partings: Eight of Cups, Three of Swords, Five of Swords, Two of Pentacles

Heartache, Disappointment: Ten of Swords, Five of Cups, Three of Swords

Money: Ace of Pentacles, Four of Pentacles, Ten of Pentacles, Page of Pentacles,
Legal Matters, Justice, and Judgment: Seven of Swords

Victory and Achievement: The Chariot, The Sun, Six of Wands

Travel: The Knights, Eight of Wands, Six of Swords, The Chariot

Spiritual Interests: The High Priestess, The Hermit, The Moon,
The Hierophant

New Enterprises: The Magician, The Fool, The Ace of Swords

Working Partnerships: Two of any suit, The Lovers

Creativity: Page of Cups, Ace of Cups, Ace of Wands, Seven of Wands

Sacrifice: The Hanged Man

The Thoth Queen

ABOVE: *Two cards of any suit show that a fruitful working partnership is about to begin.*

Make the Tarot Your Own

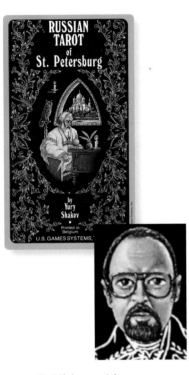

ABOVE: *Yuri Shakov created the Russian Tarot. It was painted to the exact size of reproduction, so it was sometimes necessary to use a magnifying glass.*

TOP: *Some of the details on the Russian Tarot are so fine that they had to be painted with a brush of a single hair.*

BE INSPIRED

The variety of Tarot decks is inspirational in itself. The Russian Tarot, created by Yuri Shakov, is painted to exact size, sometimes with a brush that had only a single hair. Shakov used an arm brace to steady his hand and a magnifying glass to view his work. The creators of the Motherpeace Tarot, Vicki Noble and Karen Vogel, were so inspired by a different vision of the Tarot that they recreated the 78 cards in a radical new image. In his own time Aleister Crowley was just as inspired. He and Freida Harris worked for five years to make their vision a reality. The continuing flood of contemporary Tarot speaks for the endless creativity it inspires.

The Tarot emerged as part of an age that was finding a new source of inspiration in the legacy of the classical past. We, too, are part of an age seeking vitality and reinvigoration from the past. The Tarot can open a doorway to the same classical and ancient sources that so refreshed our creative forbears, in which the gods of the ancient world become images for contemplation. In the Empress we find Demeter and Venus; in the Star we find Nuit; in the High Priestess we find Isis. Through the Empress we discover Nature and Love; through the Star we discover the Cosmos; through Isis we discover Holy Wisdom. These are, of course, the qualities that might currently serve our own cultural and spiritual rebirth.

BE CREATIVE

The Tarot has inspired works of art, music, poetry, theater and dance, collage, photomontage and computer graphics, story, history, and tapestry. The engraver Durer, the surrealist artist Salvador Dali, and the visionary mystic poet William Blake have all been inspired by it. Think of the Tarot as a deep well that leads to the collected history of us all. Whenever you draw up from the Tarot, you draw up enriched waters that perhaps you would like to share with the world, or just your family and friends. It would be a mistake to limit your creative possibilities with suggestions. This is not the place for guidelines, but for experiment.

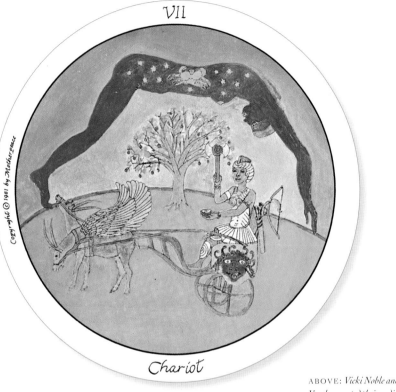

ABOVE: *Vicki Noble and Karen Vogel converted their radical vision of the Tarot into a new, distinctive circular form.*

ABOVE: *Studying the Tarot may lead you toward finding out more about other ancient divinatory sciences.*

Creativity springs from the imagination. The image and the imagination are closely connected. Feed the mind with images, and the imagination will come to life. Words alone do not have the power to stimulate this facility. Where better to find a source of meaningful universal images than in the picture book of wisdom that is the Tarot?

BE YOURSELF

Whatever you do with the Tarot, follow your own interests and develop your own gifts. If you have kept a Tarot journal, you will already have come to know yourself better. Already it should be full of your thoughts, ideas, and inspiration. Let these lead you. What aspects have you found most interesting? The Tarot as meditation, for divination, as entry into history, numerology, sacred geometry, psychology, astrology, mythology, or Qabalah? Just follow your heart. It will lead you where you need to be.

ABOVE: *Learning more about your spiritual side through the Tarot will stimulate imagination and creativity.*

Healing and the Tarot

ABOVE: *Just as a seed has the potential to grow into a towering tree, so Tarot can bring rich rewards and healing insights.*

BELOW: *Tarot provides a panoramic vision, in tune with modern ideas of global awareness and responsibility.*

MOVING FORWARD

Perhaps you came to the Tarot from curiosity. Perhaps you came to the Tarot for no particular reason whatsoever. But you came nonetheless, and hopefully you have been enriched in some way. Now that your journey with the Tarot has begun, where do you want to go from here? Every seed, no matter how small and insignificant, has the potential to bring a great future harvest. Do not underestimate the value of the seeds that you have discovered in the Tarot pack. These seeds have the power to heal.

As we move over the millennium threshold, the world is in need of healing. The 21st century beckons. How shall we measure up to new challenges? It seems only fitting that the final Tarot trump is that of the World. We are moving toward a global awareness. We are learning to develop a global consciousness. Many people believe that we are living in a time of transition between the ages, when everything is in a state of flux and redefinition. Like the world dancer who is never still, our everyday lives seem to turn increasingly faster. We, too, are in a spin.

The Tarot does not just provide a means of divination, popular though this is. It gives us ideas and symbols. Ideas are immensely powerful. Ideas have seized nations, reshaped history, and changed lives. Ideas can heal; symbols can heal. What new ideas have you found in the Tarot? What new symbols have you discovered? Have you felt empowered by these new realizations?

World Tree

XXI

The World

ABOVE: *Learn to think symbolically, stretching your imagination to enhance your appreciation of the world around you.*

HEALING THE HEART

The Tarot offers a spiritual philosophy to a Western generation looking for meaning. Meaning is healing. To live without meaning is soul-destroying. The Tarot affirms our worth. It affirms the value of our journey. It affirms our place in relation to a greater whole.

We are the products of a generation that has been educated from the head, taught to think logically and rationally, not subjectively, and certainly not imaginatively. Cerebral thinking is a fair tool, but a poor master. The Tarot reminds us how to think symbolically. This is a whole way of responding that includes the imagination and touches our sense of connection to everything. This is the seed of heart thinking. This is the seed of living holistically. This is the seed of a way of life that heals. We have touched but briefly on the fullness of the Tarot journey. So much more awaits us. Let us close with a shared meditation.

FINDING YOUR HEART'S DESIRE

Take your preferred version of Tarot trump XXI, the World. Have it in front of you and become familiar with it. Enter a meditative state and recreate the image in your imagination. As you deepen your meditation, feel your heart opening. Take the image of the world and place it in your heart. Feel love, goodwill, kindness, and peace flowing through you out to the world. Send your love as light wherever you can – to a place, a person, or a group. If you feel your heart respond, then you have touched your heart's desire.

XXI

THE WORLD

ABOVE: *Keep a mental snapshot of the World in your heart of hearts, to remind you of your connection to the planet and your fellow humans.*

Index